IRREGULAR VERBS : THE ULTIMATE GUIDE

THAT'S EASY...JUST PRACTISE!

BRYANFELDMANBOOKS@GMAIL.COM
WWW.FACEBOOK.COM/IRREGULARVERBSGUIDE

COPYRIGHT © BRYAN FELDMAN 2019
Irregular Verbs: The Ultimate Guide

All rights reserved. No portion of this book may be reproduced, stored in a retrieval system, or transmitted in any form or by any means—eletronic, mechanical, photocopy, recording, scanning, or other—except for brief quotations in critical reviews or articles, without the prior written permission of the author.

Cover and Interior Design By:
SGuerra Design

Drawings:
Freepik.com
Flaticon.com

CONTENTS

INTRODUCTION 11
   Past Simple Tense 14
   Past Simple Key Words 15
   Present Perfect Simple Tense 16
   Present Perfect Simple Key Words 17
   Note 17

Unit 1 – BE 19
   1. BE WAS/WERE BEEN 21

Unit 2 – BEAT/ BECOME/BEGIN/BITE/BLOW 27
   2. BEAT BEAT BEATEN 28
   3. BECOME BECAME BECOME 29
   4. BEGIN BEGAN BEGUN 30
   5. BITE BIT BITTEN 31
   6. BLOW BLEW BLOWN 32

Unit 3 – BREAK/BRING/ BUILD/ BUY/CATCH 37
   7. BREAK BROKE BROKEN 38
   8. BRING BROUGHT BROUGHT 39
   9. BUILD BUILT BUILT 40
   10. BUY BOUGHT BOUGHT 41
   11. CATCH CAUGHT CAUGHT 42

Unit 4 – CHOOSE/COME/COST/CUT/DO — 47
    12. CHOOSE CHOSE CHOSEN — 48
    13. COME CAME COME — 49
    14. COST COST COST — 50
    15. CUT CUT CUT — 51
    16. DO DID DONE — 52

Unit 5 – DRAW/DRINK/DRIVE/EAT/FALL — 57
    17. DRAW DREW DRAWN — 58
    18. DRINK DRANK DRUNK — 59
    19. DRIVE DROVE DRIVEN — 60
    20. EAT ATE EATEN — 61
    21. FALL FELL FALLEN — 62

Unit 6 – FEEL/ FIGHT/ FIND/FLY/FORGET — 67
    22. FEEL FELT FELT — 68
    23. FIGHT FOUGHT FOUGHT — 69
    24. FIND FOUND FOUND — 70
    25. FLY FLEW FLOWN — 71
    26. FORGET FORGOT FORGOTTEN — 72

Unit 7 – FORGIVE/GET/GIVE/GO/GROW — 77
    27. FORGIVE FORGAVE FORGIVEN — 78
    28. GET GOT GOT — 79
    29. GIVE GAVE GIVEN — 80
    30. GO WENT GONE — 81
    31. GROW GREW GROWN — 82

Unit 8 – HANG/HAVE/HEAR/HIDE/HIT   87

   32. HANG HUNG HUNG   88
   33. HAVE HAD HAD   89
   34. HEAR HEARD HEARD   90
   35. HIDE HID HIDDEN   91
   36. HIT HIT HIT   92

Unit 9 – HOLD/HURT/KEEP/KNOW/LEAVE   97

   37. HOLD HELD HELD   98
   38. HURT HURT HURT   99
   39. KEEP KEPT KEPT   100
   40. KNOW KNEW KNOWN   101
   41. LEAVE LEFT LEFT   102

Unit 10 – LEND/LET/LIE/LIGHT/LOSE   107

   42. LEND LENT LENT   108
   43. LET LET LET   109
   44. LIE LAY LAIN   110
   45. LIGHT LIT LIT   111
   46. LOSE LOST LOST   112

Unit 11 – MAKE/MEAN/MEET/PAY/PUT   117

   47. MAKE MADE MADE   118
   48. MEAN MEANT MEANT   119
   49. MEET MET MET   120
   50. PAY PAID PAID   121
   51. PUT PUT PUT   122

UNIT 12 – READ/RIDE/RING/RISE/RUN — 127
- 52. READ READ READ — 128
- 53. RIDE RODE RIDDEN — 129
- 54. RING RANG RUNG — 130
- 55. RISE ROSE RISEN — 131
- 56. RUN RAN RUN — 132

UNIT 13 – SAY/SEE/SELL/SEND/SET — 137
- 57. SAY SAID SAID — 138
- 58. SEE SAW SEEN — 139
- 59. SELL SOLD SOLD — 140
- 60. SEND SENT SENT — 141
- 61. SET SET SET — 142

UNIT 14 – SHAKE/ SHINE/SHOOT/SHOW/SHUT — 147
- 62. SHAKE SHOOK SHAKEN — 148
- 63. SHINE SHONE SHONE — 149
- 64. SHOOT SHOT SHOT — 150
- 65. SHOW SHOWED SHOWN — 151
- 66. SHUT SHUT SHUT — 152

UNIT 15 – SING/SIT/SLEEP/SPEAK/SPEND — 157
- 67. SING SANG SUNG — 158
- 68. SIT SAT SAT — 159
- 69. SLEEP SLEPT SLEPT — 160
- 70. SPEAK SPOKE SPOKEN — 161
- 71. SPEND SPENT SPENT — 162

UNIT 16 – STAND/ STEAL/STRIKE/SWIM/TAKE   167
  72. STAND STOOD STOOD   168
  73. STEAL STOLE STOLEN   169
  74. STRIKE STRUCK STRUCK   170
  75. SWIM SWAM SWUM   171
  76. TAKE TOOK TAKEN   172

UNIT 17 – TEACH/TEAR/TELL/THINK/THROW   177
  77. TEACH TAUGHT TAUGHT   178
  78. TEAR TORE TORN   179
  79. TELL TOLD TOLD   180
  80. THINK THOUGHT THOUGHT   181
  81. THROW THREW THROWN   182

UNIT 18 – UNDERSTAND/WAKE/WEAR/WIN/WRITE   187
  82. UNDERSTAND UNDERSTOOD UNDERSTOOD   188
  83. WAKE WOKE WOKEN   189
  84. WEAR WORE WORN   190
  85. WIN WON WON   191
  86. WRITE WROTE WRITTEN   192

KEY TO EXERCISES   207
ADDITIONAL EXERCISES   223
LIST OF IRREGULAR VERBS   227

INTRODUCTION

INTRODUCTION

Irregular Verbs: The Ultimate Guide is for students of English who need to learn and practise the most commonly used irregular verbs. It was written as a self-study material, but teachers will find it suitable for use in class. Both students and teachers of English will also find the book useful for revision and consolidation.

The irregular verbs are arranged in alphabetical order and there are 18 units in the book. All irregular verbs approached are classified as very frequent words in the sixth edition of the renowned *Longman Dictionary of Contemporary English*. The first unit focuses exclusively on the verb *to be*. Because of its uncommon conjugation, it was approached separately. Each following unit consists of a group of five verbs. The *Pay Attention* section presents five example sentences in the past simple tense and five example sentences in the present perfect simple tense. The *Practice Makes Perfect* section brings exercises about such verb tenses. It's worth mentioning that the past participle forms are used to make the perfect tenses and all the passive forms. The *Additional Exercises* section (pages 197-205) provides more activities to practise the past simple and past participle forms of the main irregular verbs in English. Students may check their answers by looking at the *Key to Exercises* at the back of the book.

Irregular verbs play a vital role in the English language. They make up only 3.6% of the verbs, but they outnumber the frequency of regular verbs in spoken and written English. It's also important to point out that the ten most commonly used verbs in English are irregular. The list includes *be, come, do, have, get, go, know, make, see* and *take*. The mastery of irregular verbs is crucial for those students who intend to achieve a high level of proficiency in English.

Remember! Regular verbs end with *-ed* in the past simple and past participle forms. *Ask* becomes *asked*, *paint* becomes *painted*, *love* becomes *loved*, *talk* becomes *talked*, etc. However the past simple and past participle of irregular verbs don't follow the *-ed* pattern:

BUY	BRING	CUT	GO	TAKE
BOUGHT	BROUGHT	CUT	WENT	TOOK
BOUGHT	BROUGHT	CUT	GONE	TAKEN

PAST SIMPLE TENSE

MAIN IDEA: Completed actions and events in the past time.
FORM: Regular Verbs = Verb + -ed / Irregular Verbs = Verb + Irregular Verb Forms.

We use the past simple tense:

1) to talk about events in the past that are now finished.

It was hot, so I opened the windows and took off my coat.
Alexander joined the company in 1992.

2) **to talk about habits in the past.**

He often went to night clubs at weekends when he was young.

3) **to talk about situations in the past.**

She hated mathematics when she was at the primary school.

4) **in reported speech.**

They said they would protest against the decision.

PAST SIMPLE KEY WORDS

Yesterday/ yesterday morning,
last Sunday/ last week/last month,
on Monday/on Thursday,
in January/ in March/in June,
a few minutes ago/ some days ago/two months ago,
from 1888 to 1897, from 1957 to 1971/from 1997 to 2009,
in 1504/ in 1722/ in 1912/ in 2003,
at 5 o'clock, at 9.45, etc.

PRESENT PERFECT SIMPLE TENSE

MAIN IDEA: Connects the past with the present.
FORM : Have / Has + Past Participle.
We use the Present Perfect Simple:

1) **when we are describing situations that have continued from some time in the past until now.**

   Derek has lived in Bangkok for seven years.

2) **when we are describing recent events.**

   She has just drunk two cups of tea.

3) **when we are describing repeated actions that have continued from some time in the past until now.**

   They have been to many different countries since they started dating each other.

4) **to talk about experience, that is, things that have happened at some time in our lives.**

   I've been to Berlin three times.
   Have you ever been sailing?

5) **when we can see a present result of past actions.**

   Piers has forgot the map at home and now they are completely lost.

BRYAN FELDMAN

6) when we talk about our first, second, etc. experience of something.

That's the first time Nancy has tried mountain climbing.

7) when we use the superlative.

Gina is the prettiest woman I've ever seen.

PRESENT PERFECT SIMPLE KEY WORDS

Just, already, yet, still, ever, never, for three days/ for two months/ for five years/
since Wednesday/ since 11 o'clock/ since 1997/ since she was a teenager/
so far, recently, lately
How long...+ Present Perfect Simple (How long have they been here?)
Once/twice/ three times,
This week, this month, etc.

 **NOTE**

The following verbs can be regular or irregular and were not included in the book:
burn / burned or burnt
dream / dreamed or dreamt
learn / learned or learnt
smell / smelled or smelt

1. BE WAS/WERE BEEN

> **PAY ATTENTION!**
> READ CAREFULLY THE FOLLOWING SENTENCES IN THE PAST SIMPLE.

It **was** your great chance to win the game.
The accident **wasn't** near downtown.
Those machines **weren't** broken two days ago.
Was she sick last week?
My parents **were** in New Zealand in 1996.

> **PAY ATTENTION!**
> READ CAREFULLY THE FOLLOWING SENTENCES IN THE PRESENT PERFECT SIMPLE.

We **have been** to Spain twice.
How long **have** you **been** here?
I **have been** too busy since I started working as a salesperson.
It **hasn't been** cold in some parts of the country.
My colleagues **haven't been** very helpful.

PRACTICE MAKES PERFECT

1.1 Complete the sentences using the past simple of the verb <u>To Be</u>.

a) She _____ angry yesterday.

b) The floor _____ dirty.

c) Mario and Monika _____ at home when I phoned them.

d) It _____ very hot this morning.

e) They _____ here last month.

f) My oldest sister _____ in Australia in 2006.

g) Melissa _____ the girl who lent me the coursebook.

h) They _____ at the park around 9 o'clock.

i) Jeff and Wilson _____ in Ibiza last weekend.

j) Ramon _____ the guy who helped us.

1.2 Turn these sentences into the interrogative form.

a) Susan and Ashley were close friends.

   _____?

b) The packages were heavy.

   _____?

c) Carol was very interested in politics.

   _____?

d) The shops were closed at lunchtime.

   _____?

e) Jim and Morgan were excellent golf players.

   _____?

1.3 Turn these sentences into the negative form.

   a) Your lipstick was in your bag.
   _____

   b) Nina and Naomi were well-dressed.
   _____

   c) It was a magic day for all of them.
   _____

   d) Michael and Kate were together celebrating the New Year.
   _____

   e) Nadia was a very rational person.
   _____

Now check your answers by looking at the *Key to Exercises*.

1.4 Complete the sentences with the present perfect simple of the verb <u>To Be</u>.

   a) How many times _____ you _____ to South Africa?

   b) The concert _____ a tremendous success.

   c) She (not) _____ grateful for our support.

   d) How long _____ Ronald _____ here?

   e) They (not) _____ satisfied with the latest results.

   f) Robert's father _____ to Russia three times this year.

g) I _____ never _____ to Italy.

h) There _____ some problems with the TV set.

i) _____ Clarice ever _____ to China?

j) The weather (not) _____ nice recently.

k) Carol and I (not) _____ optimistic about the future of the economy.

l) Gloria _____ unhappy since she got divorced.

m) There _____ a parade in Kennedy Street.

n) They _____ frank with us.

o) Ted _____ rude to his flatmate.

Now check your answers by looking at the *Key to Exercises*.

UNIT 2
BEAT/ BECOME/BEGIN/ BITE/BLOW

2. BEAT BEAT BEATEN

PAY ATTENTION!
READ CAREFULLY THE FOLLOWING SENTENCES IN THE PAST SIMPLE.

The Swedish company **beat** its competitors.

Matthew **beat** me at chess yesterday evening.

The police officers **beat** some demonstrators.

We felt sad when Martina **beat** the French tennis player.

Poland **beat** Italy by 4 – 2 on Friday.

PAY ATTENTION!
READ CAREFULLY THE FOLLOWING SENTENCES IN THE PRESENT PERFECT SIMPLE.

Manchester **has beaten** Arsenal again.

George **hasn't beaten** the world record yet.

The government **has beaten** the inflation over the last decade.

Have you **beaten** the eggs?

The powerful politicians **have beaten** their opponents.

3. BECOME BECAME BECOME

PAY ATTENTION!
READ CAREFULLY THE FOLLOWING SENTENCES IN THE PAST SIMPLE.

The band **became** popular in the 1990s.
George V **became** king on 6 May 1910.
Star Wars **became** a blockbuster in 1977.
Taking care of the children **became** my priority two years ago.
The theory **became** known at the end of the 19th century.

PAY ATTENTION!
READ CAREFULLY THE FOLLOWING SENTENCES IN THE PRESENT PERFECT SIMPLE.

Peter **has become** a loving father over the past few months.
Robert and Hillary **haven't become** the best lawyers in town.
It **has become** difficult to understand Sherman's behaviour.
Why **have** you **become** so impatient with Melinda?
Allan **has** never **become** a successful engineer.

4. BEGIN BEGAN BEGUN

PAY ATTENTION!
READ CAREFULLY THE FOLLOWING SENTENCES IN THE PAST SIMPLE.

In the second year students **began** the study of German.
My daughter **began** teaching in 2004.
The baseball match **began** ten minutes late.
David **began** criticising everyone around him.
Steven Spielberg **began** the film career in 1975.

PAY ATTENTION!
READ CAREFULLY THE FOLLOWING SENTENCES IN THE PRESENT PERFECT SIMPLE.

Audrey **has** already **begun** learning to drive.
The graphic design course **hasn't begun** yet.
Have you **begun** writing the poem?
Mary **has begun** taking singing lessons lately.
Peter and I **have begun** getting in touch with our clients.

5. BITE BIT BITTEN

PAY ATTENTION!
READ CAREFULLY THE FOLLOWING SENTENCES IN THE PAST SIMPLE.

A snake **bit** Rudy as he was walking through the woods.
Stephania **bit** her lips when she felt anxious.
Dennis **bit** off a big chunk of meat.
Eric **bit** into the peach.
An insect **bit** the baby's cheeks some minutes ago.

PAY ATTENTION!
READ CAREFULLY THE FOLLOWING SENTENCES IN THE PRESENT PERFECT SIMPLE.

Liz **has bitten** into the cotton candy.
The little boy **has bitten** his tongue.
The dog **has bitten** my ankle.
Mosquitoes **have bitten** us badly all day long!
I **have** just **bitten** a delicious piece of pizza.

6. BLOW BLEW BLOWN

PAY ATTENTION!
READ CAREFULLY THE FOLLOWING SENTENCES IN THE PAST SIMPLE.

My cap **blew** away, but I didn't run after it.
Shirley got angry when Andy **blew** smoke into her face.
It **blew** really hard last night.
Fred **blew** bubbles in the backyard.
I took a handkerchief and **blew** my nose.

PAY ATTENTION!
READ CAREFULLY THE FOLLOWING SENTENCES IN THE PRESENT PERFECT SIMPLE.

It **has blown** from the southeast direction.
The wind **has blown** the dust into the house.
Gina's hair **has blown** in the sea breeze.
I **have blown** into my tea to cool it down.
Suddenly the motor **has blown** up!

PRACTICE MAKES PERFECT

2.1 Complete the sentences with the past simple of the verbs in the box below. Use each verb twice.

| BEAT | BECOME | BEGIN | BITE | BLOW |

a) At last Daisy _____ familiar with the local customs.

b) While Lyla watched *The Others*, she _____ the nails all the time.

c) Collin _____ stress by doing yoga.

d) The air _____ through the open doors.

e) By the end of the trip they _____ feeling bored.

f) The strong wind _____ down the trees.

g) Glenda _____ jealous of her husband.

h) Luke _____ complaining about the hotel services.

i) I _____ a cookie and drank some tea.

j) Someone _____ on the door.

2.2 Turn these sentences into the interrogative form.

a) He beat Andrew in the last swimming race.

_____?

b) Alice became curious about astrology.

_____?

c) The meeting began on time.

_____?

d) The dog bit Sylvia on the arm.

_____?

e) Arnold blew out the candles.

_____?

2.3 Turn these sentences into the negative form.

   a) They beat us in the final round of the world championship.
   _____

   b) Sandra became a top model in 2015.
   _____

   c) The interview began at 9 a.m.
   _____

   d) Margaux bit the doughnut slowly.
   _____

   e) Dorothy blew up the yellow balloons.
   _____

Now check your answers by looking at the *Key to Exercises*.

2.4 Complete the sentences with the present perfect simple of the verbs in brackets.

   a) Our prices (beat) _____ yours!

   b) The town (become) _____ home to a car museum.

   c) Karl (begin) _____ his musical career as a drummer.

   d) The hamster (bite) _____ a piece of cheese.

   e) The referee (blow) _____ the whistle for the second half.

   f) I (beat/ not) _____ Phill at poker yet.

g) Paula and Mirian (become) _____ just _____ Canadian citizens.

h) Daise and Don (begin) _____ playing with some puppets.

i) Tammy (bite/not) _____ the apple before washing it.

j) The tyres (blow) _____ out on my way to work.

k) (beat) _____ Russia _____ the favourite team?

l) Jane's dreams (become) _____ possible thanks to a stroke of luck.

m) (begin) _____ the lecture _____ yet?

n) I (bite) _____ a slice of jelly roll.

o) The tall fence (blow) _____ over in the storm.

Now check your answers by looking at the Key to Exercises.

UNIT 3
BREAK/BRING/ BUILD/ BUY/CATCH

7. BREAK BROKE BROKEN

PAY ATTENTION!
READ CAREFULLY THE FOLLOWING SENTENCES IN THE PAST SIMPLE.

As Josh and Faye **broke** the law, they were punished.

I was checking the papers when Bill **broke** my concentration.

I **broke** a brandy glass while I was doing the dishes.

Theresa **broke** the croissant in two and handed one piece to Russel.

My youngest brother **broke** my mobile phone screen some days ago.

PAY ATTENTION!
READ CAREFULLY THE FOLLOWING SENTENCES IN THE PRESENT PERFECT SIMPLE.

Have the children **broken** the vases?

Gerald **has broken** his left leg in two places.

Someone **has broken** the washing machine recently.

My truck **has broken down** twice this month.

Janet and Sean started talking and **have broken** the silence.

8. BRING BROUGHT BROUGHT

PAY ATTENTION!
READ CAREFULLY THE FOLLOWING SENTENCES IN THE PAST SIMPLE.

It was a rainy day, so Lucy **brought** an umbrella.
Luckily she **brought** good news to everyone.
Chuck **brought** some friends to have dinner with us on Wednesday.
Klaus **brought** a carton of mango juice and fresh fruits to the brunch.
Last year the company **brought** hundreds of jobs to San Diego.

PAY ATTENTION!
READ CAREFULLY THE FOLLOWING SENTENCES IN THE PRESENT PERFECT SIMPLE.

Your presence **has brought** us hope and excitement over the last weeks.
So far Susan **hasn't brought** the ingredients that we need.
Has the waiter **brought** the bill?
Thomson **has brought** something back for you.
The pictures **have brought** back a lot of childhood memories.

9. BUILD BUILT BUILT

> **PAY ATTENTION!**
> READ CAREFULLY THE FOLLOWING SENTENCES IN THE PAST SIMPLE.

The sparrows **built** their nest under the roof of the temple.

Jack **built** his own house ten years ago.

The billionaire **built** a skyscraper in the city centre.

Gloria and I **built** a tree house to the kids.

The girls **built** a sandcastle while they were playing on the beach.

> **PAY ATTENTION!**
> READ CAREFULLY THE FOLLOWING SENTENCES IN THE PRESENT PERFECT SIMPLE.

We **have built** a fire to warm us up.

They still **haven't built** a bridge to join the two historical towns.

Lawrence **has built** an amazing reputation as a plastic surgeon.

Have they **built** the new road already?

The two priests **have built** a magnificent church.

10. BUY BOUGHT BOUGHT

PAY ATTENTION!
READ CAREFULLY THE FOLLOWING SENTENCES IN THE PAST SIMPLE.

Peter **bought** spices and herbs in the supermarket.
I **bought** my girlfriend a bunch of flowers.
George **bought** a leather jacket and a pair of tennis shoes.
Ricky **bought** a wonderful painting some months ago.
Walden **bought** a bottle of French perfume in the shopping centre.

PAY ATTENTION!
READ THE FOLLOWING SENTENCES IN THE PRESENT PERFECT SIMPLE.

The Dutch Formula one racing driver **has bought** a BMW.
Where **have** you **bought** that jumper?
I **haven't bought** my tickets yet.
They **have bought** a penthouse near Central Park.
Rachel **hasn't bought** winter clothes for ages.

11. CATCH CAUGHT CAUGHT

PAY ATTENTION!
READ CAREFULLY THE FOLLOWING SENTENCES IN THE PAST SIMPLE.

I **caught** the last train to my hometown at 10.45 p.m.
Howard and Pat **caught** their grandson smoking.
Your question **caught** me by surprise.
The building **caught** fire three years ago.
My son **caught** the ball and started running.

PAY ATTENTION!
READ CAREFULLY THE FOLLOWING SENTENCES IN THE PRESENT PERFECT SIMPLE.

My grandfather **has caught** the flu again.
My explanation was really interesting. I **have caught** everyone's attention!
Have the police **caught** the thieves yet?
Andrew **hasn't caught** the beginning of the musical.
Just as Drew turned around, she **has caught** Errol flirting with Meredith.

PRACTICE MAKES PERFECT

3.1 Complete the sentences with the past simple of the verbs in the box below. Use each verb twice.

| BREAK | BRING | BUILD | BUY | CATCH |

a) The fire fighters _____ the victims to a safe place.

b) Luciano _____ the Land Rover for $80,000.

c) Helen's car _____ down in the tunnel half an hour ago.

d) Elaine _____ the matter to an end.

e) He was a pacifist who _____ bridges between the two nations.

f) Wanderson _____ measles from his classmate last term.

g) Thieves _____ into Patrick's house on Thursday.

h) While I was listening to a song by U2, I _____ myself thinking of Roy.

i) Stuart _____ the kettle for $100.

j) Craig _____ a wall safe to keep the sculptures.

3.2 Turn these sentences into the interrogative form.

a) The printer broke down again.
_____?

b) The research brought a fresh look to the topic.
_____?

c) They built the cathedral in the 18th century.
_____?

d) Josh bought a gold bracelet.
_____?

e) The FBI agents caught the terrorists.
_____?

3.3 Turn these sentences into the negative form.

a) Will broke his middle finger.

    _____.

b) Pablo brought home his Portuguese workmates.

    _____.

c) They built a luxury hotel near the sports centre.

    _____.

d) Sophia bought Karen a nightdress.

    _____.

e) Claudia and Britney caught a movie the other day.

    _____.

Now check your answers by looking at the *Key to Exercises*.

3.4 Complete the sentences with the present perfect simple of the verbs in brackets.

a) Melissa dropped the jar and (break) _____ it.

b) My comments (bring) _____ happiness to the children.

c) She (build/not) still _____ many friendships at college.

d) We (buy) _____ many gifts for our friends.

e) *Harry Potter* is a story that (catch) _____ the imagination of readers all over the world since it was published.

f) Sabrina (break) _____ the habit of cheating in the tests.

g) Such bad memories (bring) _____ tears to my eyes.

h) Peter (build) _____ Karen a doll's house.

i) Werner sold his motorbike and (buy) _____ a comfortable car.

j) The eagle (catch) _____ the fish.

k) After a misunderstanding, Anita (break) _____ up with me.

l) (bring) _____ you _____ more vanilla ice-cream?

m) The foundation (build) _____ thousands of houses for poor families in African countries.

n) The ties were on sale, but I (buy /not) _____ them.

o) (catch) _____ the cat _____ the little bird?

Now check your answers by looking at the *Key to Exercises*.

12. CHOOSE CHOSE CHOSEN

> **PAY ATTENTION!**
> READ CAREFULLY THE FOLLOWING SENTENCES IN THE PAST SIMPLE.

I **chose** Jake for doing the job.
Derek **chose** to learn Italian rather than Spanish.
The company **chose** its new director in March.
Norma **chose** the words carefully to write an article about self-esteem.
I **chose** to keep as much distance as possible from such dangerous people.

> **PAY ATTENTION!**
> READ CAREFULLY THE FOLLOWING SENTENCES IN THE PRESENT PERFECT SIMPLE.

Karen **has chosen** to invest the money in the real estate market.
I'm sure they **haven't chosen** the best athlete to represent us.
Have they **chosen** their leader?
We **have chosen** to watch a comedy to have some fun.
She **has** already **chosen** a purple scarf from the many in the closet.

13. COME CAME COME

PAY ATTENTION!
READ CAREFULLY THE FOLLOWING SENTENCES IN THE PAST SIMPLE.

The defeat **came** at the worst possible time.
The dentist **came** into the waiting room impatiently.
Peter **came** here the day before yesterday.
Roy and Amanda **came** to the theatre early.
He **came** first in the car race.

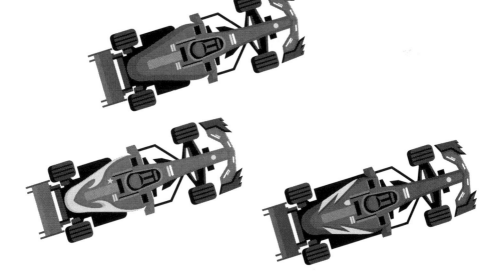

PAY ATTENTION!
READ CAREFULLY THE FOLLOWING SENTENCES IN THE PRESENT PERFECT SIMPLE.

Louis **hasn't come** to see his parents since he moved to the countryside.
Have you **come** to any conclusion?
I **have come** to help you!
Michael and Christina **have come** a long way to visit us.
Nicole **has** just **come** back to the office.

14. COST COST COST

PAY ATTENTION!
READ CAREFULLY THE FOLLOWING SENTENCES IN THE PAST SIMPLE.

It **cost** him a few thousand pounds to make his dream come true.
I don't know how much the royal wedding party **cost.**
Each cotton cushion **cost** $90.
At the time computers were enormous, complicated and **cost** a great deal of money.
I didn't buy the watch I wanted because it **cost** a small fortune.

PAY ATTENTION!
READ CAREFULLY THE FOLLOWING SENTENCES IN THE PRESENT PERFECT SIMPLE.

Making the arrangements **has cost** me a full day's work.
Such silly mistakes **have cost** your promotion!
So far it **hasn't cost** lots of money to repair the monument.
My earrings **haven't cost** as much as you might suppose.
The movie **has cost** $40.000.000.

15. CUT CUT CUT

PAY ATTENTION!
READ CAREFULLY THE FOLLOWING SENTENCES IN THE PAST SIMPLE.

Bruce works for a company that **cut** costs in the first quarter of the year.
Virginia **cut** the fashion magazine with an old pair of scissors.
Whitney **cut** the lemon in half.
Crystal **cut** and pasted the text some minutes ago.
The hairdresser **cut** Polly's hair short.

PAY ATTENTION!
READ CAREFULLY THE FOLLOWING SENTENCES IN THE PRESENT PERFECT SIMPLE.

I **have cut** the carrots and tomatoes into small dices.
Gavin **has cut** a chunk of meat with a sharp knife.
Have you **cut** the onions?
George **has** already **cut** the grass.
Iris **has cut** me a slice of brown bread.

16. DO DID DONE

PAY ATTENTION!
READ CAREFULLY THE FOLLOWING SENTENCES IN THE PAST SIMPLE.

Hillary **did** the cleaning very fast.
I'm sure Tony **did** his best to pass the entrance exam.
Piers **did** the same exercises day in day out to lose weight.
We **did** business with the South African investors at the end of October.
Claire **did** the housework in the afternoon.

PAY ATTENTION!
READ CAREFULLY THE FOLLOWING SENTENCES IN THE PRESENT PERFECT SIMPLE.

Brendon **has** never **done** anything for his community.
Victor and Angelina **haven't done** their homework yet.
What **have** you **done** with my hair brush?
Sharon **has** just **done** you a great favour.
Writing a book **has done** wonders for me.

PRACTICE MAKES PERFECT !

4.1 Complete the sentences with the past simple of the verbs in the box. Use each verb twice.

| CHOOSE | COME | COST | CUT | DO |

a) I _____ down sugar from my diet six months ago.

b) The publishing house _____ Los Angeles as its base.

c) Natasha _____ what she could to spread the word about the benefits of recycling.

d) Judy _____ across a family album at the bottom of a trunk.

e) The rucksack _____ one hundred euros.

f) Graham _____ badly trying to be a politician.

g) Joe _____ himself when he started shaving.

h) Tatyana and Thomas had a look at the travel guide and _____ Istambul to spend their honeymoon.

i) David and Sophie _____ back after midnight.

j) The Channel Tunnel _____ $21 billion!

4.2 Turn these sentences into the interrogative form.

a) They chose to live in a quiet neighbourhood.
_____?

b) The circus came to town last spring.
_____?

c) The Easter egg cost ten pounds.
_____?

d) Beatrice cut herself chopping carrots.
_____?

e) The doctors did everything possible to save Gail.
_____?

4.3 Turn these sentences into the negative form.

a) I chose a lively wallpaper for the living room.

_____.

b) Debra came by our shop.

_____.

c) My dental treatment cost me $3,000.

_____.

d) Ellon cut precisely along the dotted lines.

_____.

e) Fred did the washing slowly.

_____.

Now check your answers by looking at the *Key to Exercises*.

4.4 Complete the sentences with the present perfect simple of the verbs in brackets.

a) We (choose/not) _____ a name for our pet yet.

b) It isn't raining any more. The sun (come) _____ finally _____ out!

c) My sunglasses (cost) _____ $50.

d) Gregory _____ (cut) across the mountains to save time.

e) Ursula (do) _____ the ironing.

IRREGULAR VERBS: THE ULTIMATE GUIDE

f) Debby (choose) _____ to stay with us until the end of the year.

g) Hillary left the room and (come) _____ never _____ back.

h) The mansion renovation (cost) _____ $1,000,000!

i) Martin (cut) _____ classes again!

j) (do) _____ Margareth _____ the cooking yet?

k) The coach (choose) _____ the new captain of the team.

l) Your suggestion (come) _____ at the best possible moment.

m) The two football players (cost) _____ Manchester United two hundred million pounds.

n) Fortunately the government (cut) _____ interest rates.

o) Frank (do) _____ the puzzle in fifteen minutes. He's such a smart boy!

Now check your answers by looking at the *Key to Exercises*.

UNIT 5
DRAW/DRINK/DRIVE/ EAT/FALL

17. DRAW DREW DRAWN

PAY ATTENTION!
READ CAREFULLY THE FOLLOWING SENTENCES IN THE PAST SIMPLE.

I **drew** a picture of the house where I lived as a child.
Marcia **drew** a palace surrounded by hills and valleys.
Felicity **drew** attention to herself because she was wearing flashy clothes.
The children **drew** Japanese and American superheroes.
Ava **drew** a pigeon and then painted it.

PAY ATTENTION!
READ CAREFULLY THE FOLLOWING SENTENCES IN THE PRESENT PERFECT SIMPLE.

Max **has drawn** a small road map.
I **haven't drawn** the picture very well.
The French journalist **has drawn** a comparison between the two political parties.
The economist **has drawn** two charts.
American films **have drawn** large audiences over the years.

18. DRINK DRANK DRUNK

PAY ATTENTION!
READ CAREFULLY THE FOLLOWING SENTENCES IN THE PAST SIMPLE.

Pauline **drank** two glasses of cashew juice.
I **drank** so much beer that I felt sick.
I'm not feeling well because I **drank** a lot yesterday.
We **drank** two cups of tea while we were having a chat.
The couple **drank** champagne and ate caviar.

PAY ATTENTION!
READ CAREFULLY THE FOLLOWING SENTENCES IN THE PRESENT PERFECT SIMPLE.

Bess' father **has drunk** too much lately.
I **haven't drunk** milk for such a long time!
Have you ever **drunk** whiskey?
I **have** just **drunk** three glasses of mineral water.
Elizabeth **has** never **drunk** alcohol.

IRREGULAR VERBS: THE ULTIMATE GUIDE

19. DRIVE DROVE DRIVEN

PAY ATTENTION!
READ CAREFULLY THE FOLLOWING SENTENCES IN THE PAST SIMPLE.

She **drove** her husband to work around 8 o'clock.

Jaqueline **drove** fast and crashed the car.

At 5.00 p.m. Marlon **drove** to school to pick up the kids.

George **drove** us crazy by telling stupid jokes.

Lorraine and Walt **drove** themselves to the University of Cambridge.

PAY ATTENTION!
READ CAREFULLY THE FOLLOWING SENTENCES IN THE PRESENT PERFECT SIMPLE.

It's the first time I **have driven** a Porsche!

So far Hans **hasn't driven** his new car.

The boss' comments **have driven** them mad.

Have you ever **driven** a bus?

Chelston **has driven** to the farm on his tractor.

20. EAT ATE EATEN

PAY ATTENTION!
READ CAREFULLY THE FOLLOWING SENTENCES IN THE PAST SIMPLE.

I **ate** fish and vegetables for lunch.

We **ate** Chinese food last Sunday.

For dessert Susan **ate** a slice of strawberry tart.

Ali and I **ate** popcorn while we watched a TV series.

All of us **ate** a lot of sweets at the party.

PAY ATTENTION!
READ CAREFULLY THE FOLLOWING SENTENCES IN THE PRESENT PERFECT SIMPLE.

Have you ever **eaten** Indian food?

Lars **has eaten** a salad with cucumber, beets and tomatoes.

Sylvester **has eaten** a light breakfast.

I **haven't eaten** Italian food recently.

We **have eaten** twice in the *Grand Restaurant* this week.

21. FALL FELL FALLEN

PAY ATTENTION!
READ CAREFULLY THE FOLLOWING SENTENCES IN THE PAST SIMPLE.

The dish **fell** from my hands.
Anne **fell** and hurt her knees.
My notebooks **fell** from the top shelf.
The two teenagers **fell** and hurt themselves.
Doris' birthday **fell** on the last Friday of February.

PAY ATTENTION!
READ CAREFULLY THE FOLLOWING SENTENCES IN THE PRESENT PERFECT SIMPLE.

The pine **has** just **fallen**.
She **has fallen** in love with Paris right away.
He was exhausted and **has fallen** asleep.
The rain **hasn't fallen** all day long.
Chris **has fallen** down the stairs!

PRACTICE MAKES PERFECT

5.1 Complete the sentences with the past simple of the verbs in the box below. Use each verb twice.

| DRAW | DRINK | DRIVE | EAT | FALL |

a) Andrew _____ home and had an early night.

b) Alice _____ a sketch of an evening dress.

c) As the weather was very hot, we _____ plenty of water.

d) My pets _____ their food quickly.

e) She slipped from the tree and _____ to the ground.

f) Zach _____ like a fish!

g) Vicky _____ shapes such as triangles, circles and squares.

h) Liz _____ spaghetti for dinner.

i) A heavy rain _____ this morning.

j) Henry _____ for miles before stopping for a rest.

5.2 Turn these sentences into the interrogative form.

a) Erika drew tropical birds.

_____?

b) Ron and Fred drank a bottle of white wine.

_____?

c) They drove back to Cardiff.

_____?

d) Joy and Raymond ate out yesterday evening.

_____?

e) Mick fell on the pavement.

_____?

5.3 Turn these sentences into the negative form.

a) Alison drew wild animals.

_____.

b) Sean drank three cups of coffee this morning.

_____.

c) Wayne drove Claire to the airport.

_____.

d) They ate a tasty fruit salad after having lunch.

_____.

e) Temperatures fell below zero in the second week of December.

_____.

5.4 Complete the sentences with the present perfect simple of the verbs in brackets.

a) The concert (draw) _____ people of different ages.

b) Frida (drink) _____ never _____ tequilla.

c) Ron (drive) _____ into the back of a coach.

d) We (eat) _____ at the *Mont Blanc Restaurant.*

e) We tried to follow the athletes, but of course we (fall) _____ behind.

f) Some of us (draw) _____ with crayons and coloured pencils.

g) Richard (drink) _____ two glasses of soft drink.

h) I (drive) _____ myself to Detroit.

i) Pauline put on weight because she (eat) _____ a lot of fatty food recently.

j) Thanks to Bruce, the report (fall/not) _____ into the wrong hands.

k) (draw) _____ you ever _____ a cartoon?

l) How many glasses of water (drink) _____ you _____ today?

m) Tom got into the car and (drive) _____ away.

IRREGULAR VERBS: THE ULTIMATE GUIDE 65

n) (eat) I _____ never _____ Thai food.

o) It's unbelievable that such a corporation _____ (fell) apart!

UNIT 6
FEEL/ FIGHT/ FIND/ FLY/FORGET

22. FEEL FELT FELT

PAY ATTENTION!
READ CAREFULLY THE FOLLOWING SENTENCES IN THE PAST SIMPLE.

The baby **felt** hungry and started crying.
After taking the medicine, I **felt** a little better.
When she received the prize, Winnie **felt** like the most special person in the world.
Marjorie **felt** that she had made a huge difference in many people's lives.
Boris **felt** overjoyed as soon as he was told about the pay rise.

PAY ATTENTION!
READ CAREFULLY THE FOLLOWING SENTENCES IN THE PRESENT PERFECT SIMPLE.

She **hasn't felt** guilty for what happened.
Have you **felt** tense about sharing the same room with Albert?
Susan **has felt** a little pressure on the shoulders.
Lexi **has felt** more secure since Luke joined the staff.
I **have felt** deeply disappointed about our relationship.

23. FIGHT FOUGHT FOUGHT

PAY ATTENTION!
READ CAREFULLY THE FOLLOWING SENTENCES IN THE PAST SIMPLE.

The country **fought** a long war in the 1980s.
She fought **with** her parents.
Nelson Mandela **fought** against injustice and repression.
Peter and Paul **fought** in Iraq in 2003.
The two boys **fought** with each other.

PAY ATTENTION!
READ CAREFULLY THE FOLLOWING SENTENCES IN THE PRESENT PERFECT SIMPLE.

They **have fought** for control of the country over the past years.
Kathlen **has** bravely **fought** for her life.
She **has fought** like a tiger to give her family emotional and financial support.
I can't believe my parents **have** already **fought** twice this week!
Have you ever **fought** for a girl?

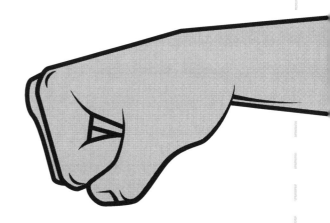

IRREGULAR VERBS: THE ULTIMATE GUIDE

24. FIND FOUND FOUND

PAY ATTENTION!
READ CAREFULLY THE FOLLOWING SENTENCES IN THE PAST SIMPLE.

I **found** some coins when I was cleaning the balcony.

They **found** themselves lost in the jungle.

We **found** the play extremely boring.

Maya **found** a handbag in the street on Tuesday.

Bob **found** Viola pretty and attractive.

PAY ATTENTION!
READ CAREFULLY THE FOLLOWING SENTENCES IN THE PRESENT PERFECT SIMPLE.

Have you **found** your pen?

She **hasn't found** a place to live yet.

I **have** just **found** the gate unlocked.

Ruth **has found** out what was wrong with the refrigerator.

They **have found** the gun by chance.

25. FLY FLEW FLOWN

PAY ATTENTION!
READ CAREFULLY THE FOLLOWING SENTENCES IN THE PAST SIMPLE.

She **flew** back to Vienna yesterday at 10.30 a.m.
The birds **flew** in the bright blue sky.
The young pilot **flew** the aircraft to Toronto.
They **flew** to Buenos Aires two days ago.
We **flew** economy class because we wanted to save money.

PAY ATTENTION!
READ CAREFULLY THE FOLOWING SENTENCES IN THE PRESENT PERFECT SIMPLE.

She **has** never **flown** before.
Have you ever **flown** a helicopter?
She **has** already **flown** to New York on business.
The birds **have flown** to the oak tree.
Sharon **has flown** to Frankfurt to make a deal.

26. FORGET FORGOT FORGOTTEN

> **PAY ATTENTION!**
> READ CAREFULLY THE FOLLOWING SENTENCES IN THE PAST SIMPLE.

You told me your address, but I **forgot**.

I **forgot** to send your email.

Anthony **forgot** about the important notice.

Sean **forgot** his wallet at home on Monday morning.

The other day Robson **forgot** the diary in the office.

> **PAY ATTENTION!**
> READ CAREFULLY THE FOLLOWING SENTENCES IN THE PRESENT PERFECT SIMPLE.

He **has** completely **forgotten** to apologize to Sue.

Have you ever **forgotten** your own birthday?

I **have forgotten** to turn off the lights.

Mark **has forgotten** the doctor's appointment.

Believe it or not Ted **has forgotten** to give Carol my message!

PRACTICE MAKES PERFECT

6.1 Complete the sentences with the past simple of the verbs below. Use each verb twice.

| FEEL | FIGHT | FIND | FLY | FORGET |

a) My feet _____ cold and rough.

b) Donald was so terrified that he _____ his own name.

c) They _____ like cat and dog.

d) The space shuttle Endeavour _____ into space for the first time in 1992.

e) In July the president _____ to Tokyo for a five-day visit.

f) Irma _____ blushing when Ronald told the joke.

g) We totally _____ to buy Brookie a gift.

h) Geraldine and I _____ all the time. After all we were so different from each other.

i) Matt travelled to Tibet and _____ out a new life style.

j) Justin _____ the chemistry worksheet very hard.

6.2 Turn these sentences into the interrogative form.

a) He felt great after the trip.
___

b) Arnold fought in Vietnam in 1971.
___

c) She found an experienced employee to replace Stan.
___

d) They flew Lufthansa.
___

e) Mel forgot to pay the phone bill.
___

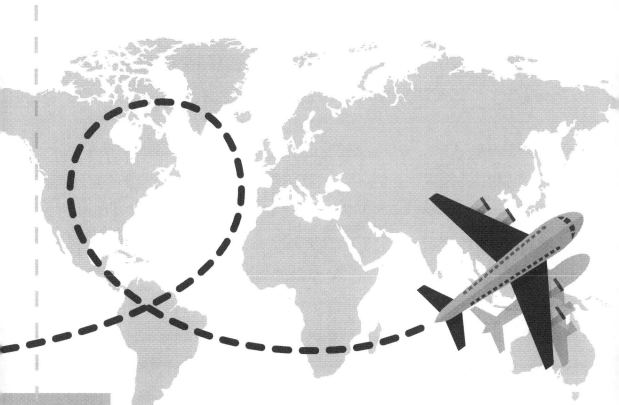

6.3 Turn these sentences into the negative form.

a) I felt relaxed after having a walk.

_____

b) Gabriel fought with his neighbour.

_____

c) I found that soap opera confusing.

_____

d) The doves flew to the north at sunrise.

_____

e) Carol and I forgot to invite Emily to the barbecue.

_____

Now check your answers by looking at the *Key to Exercises*.

6.4 Complete the sentences with the present perfect simple of the verbs in brackets.

a) Nobody (feel) _____ motivated about the project.

b) The workers (fight) _____ for better pay and conditions.

c) We (find) _____ a really good snack bar near the amusement park.

d) (fly) _____ they _____ across the Pacific Ocean?

e) (forget) _____ you _____ your passsword?

f) Harrison (feel) _____ never _____ so lucky.

g) I (fight) _____ with my mother-in-law.

h) Denis (find) _____ himself dancing jazz.

i) (fly) _____ you ever _____ a kite?

j) Lily (forget) _____ never _____ our first date.

k) I (feel) _____ relieved since Sidney became the new boss.

l) The fire brigade (fight) _____ the fire for five hours.

m) I (find) _____ two incredible pubs in Belfast!

n) They are rich, but they (fly/not) _____ first class.

o) Marylin (forget) _____ to call me back.

Now check your answers by looking at *key to Exercises*.

UNIT 7
FORGIVE/GET/GIVE/GO/GROW

27. FORGIVE FORGAVE FORGIVEN

> **PAY ATTENTION!**
> READ CAREFULLY THE FOLLOWING SENTENCES IN THE PAST SIMPLE.

Meghan **forgave** Cecil for lying to her.
Evelyn **forgave** herself for believing in such stupid promises!
I **forgave** Janet for offending me during the debate.
The United States **forgave** the Latin American country's debt.
Jim **forgave** me for being too hard on him some time ago.

> **PAY ATTENTION!**
> READ CAREFULLY THE FOLLOWING SENTENCES IN THE PRESENT PERFECT SIMPLE.

You were so selfish, but I **have** already **forgiven** you!
I **have forgiven** Karen for not helping me when I needed her most.
Victor **has forgiven** himself for not achieving his goal.
I **haven't forgiven** you for hurting my feelings.
Have you **forgiven** Marcel for hitting you?

28. GET GOT GOT

PAY ATTENTION!
READ CAREFULLY THE FOLLOWING SENTENCES IN THE PAST SIMPLE.

I **got** a shock when I saw Isabel's new look.
Jeniffer **got** top marks in the examinations.
They **got** $500.000 for their apartment.
Anna **got** married last fall.
At last she **got** a visa to work in Canada.

PAY ATTENTION!
READ CAREFULLY THE FOLLOWING SENTENCES IN THE PRESENT PERFECT SIMPLE.

Has she **got** a job yet?
The situation **has got** more and more complicated.
Herbert **hasn't got** over his financial problems.
I **have got** a lot of presents lately.
We **haven't got** any good ideas for a long time.

 **NOTE**

IN AMERICAN ENGLISH THE PAST PARTICIPLE OF THE VERB GET IS USUALLY GOTTEN.

29. GIVE GAVE GIVEN

PAY ATTENTION!
READ CAREFULLY THE FOLLOWING SENTENCES IN THE PAST SIMPLE.

After winning the award, Chesley **gave** a long speech.

The teacher **gave** us examples of classical literature.

The old lady **gave** us directions to the train station.

We **gave** Kelly a second chance.

On Wednesday I **gave** them some money to buy a hamburger.

PAY ATTENTION!
READ CAREFULLY THE FOLLOWING SENTENCES IN THE PRESENT PERFECT SIMPLE.

Oliver **has given** up smoking.

My sister **has** just **given** birth to twins.

Frank and George **have given** their parents a kiss.

I **have** already **given** you my bank account details.

Have you ever **given** a presentation?

30. GO WENT GONE

PAY ATTENTION!
READ CAREFULLY THE FOLLOWING SENTENCES IN THE PAST SIMPLE.

Liz **went** to the mall on foot half an hour ago.
She **went** for a walk around Times Square.
My parents **went** on a cruise at the end of the 1990s.
I **went** shopping with my nephew on Black Friday.
Hillary **went** to a shoe shop to buy high heeled shoes.

PAY ATTENTION!
READ CAREFULLY THE FOLLOWING SENTENCES IN THE PRESENT PERFECT SIMPLE.

They still **haven't gone** to Madrid.
Leonardo **has just** gone home.
Have you **gone** skiing lately?
They **have gone** fishing with us many times.
Angela **has gone** to the Philippines twice this year.

31. GROW GREW GROWN

> **PAY ATTENTION!**
> READ CAREFULLY THE FOLLOWING SENTENCES IN THE PAST SIMPLE.

Helmut **grew up** in Geneva.
Anderson **grew** two inches.
The old farmer **grew** tomatoes and potatoes.
My grandfather **grew** coffee many years ago.
Rotterdam **grew** along with the shipping industry.

> **PAY ATTENTION!**
> READ CAREFULLY THE FOLLOWING SENTENCES IN THE PRESENT PERFECT SIMPLE.

Sophia lives in a city which **has grown** fast.
Roman **has grown** a beard.
Such plants **haven't grown** because the region is too hot.
It's amazing how our business **has grown** over the past two years.
Have you ever **grown** tulips in your garden?

PRACTICE MAKES PERFECT

7.1 Complete the sentences with the past simple of the verbs below. Use each verb twice.

| FORGIVE | GET | GIVE | GO | GROW |

a) Edson _____ up in a very catholic family.

b) As the months _____ by, everyone became more efficient.

c) It was cloudy and windy when they _____ here.

d) Fortunately they _____ us for making such a stupid mistake!

e) Adele _____ me a very useful piece of advice.

f) The plants in my backyard _____ quickly last summer.

g) Daniel _____ swimming on Sunday morning.

h) Jakob _____ along very well with the new human resources manager.

i) She _____ back my pencil when she finished using it.

j) I _____ Wim for what he did.

7.2 Turn these sentences into the interrogative form.

a) Chris forgave his brother for such a bad behaviour.
_____?

b) Ed got a post as a marketing director.
_____?

c) The nurse gave him an injection.
_____?

d) Ryan went to a pizzeria.
_____?

e) Enrico grew up playing different sports.
_____?

7.3 Turn these sentences into the negative form.

a) Nicky forgave his girlfriend for being unfaithful to him.
_____.

b) I got on the train at Bristol station.
_____.

c) George gave the supervisor a creative solution to the problem.
_____.

d) Rachel went to the Louvre Museum twice last month.
_____.

e) The Mexican economy grew 2% in 2017.
_____.

Now check your answers by looking at the *Key to Exercises*.

7.4 Complete the sentences with the present perfect simple of the verbs in brackets.

a) I'm not sure Keith (forgive) _____ Paola for not telling the truth about her identity.

b) I really don't know how William (get) _____ the money to pay the diving lessons.

c) Professor Miles (give) _____ them a brief history of the Spanish Civil War.

d) Marjorie and Michael (go) _____ to a seaside resort near Orlando.

e) My brother and I (grow/not) _____ up together.

f) Sheila (forgive) _____ herself for not succeeding in getting a job abroad.

g) (get) _____ they _____ on very well in the intensive training course?

h) The spicy food (give) _____ me indigestion.

i) Carol and Patrick (go) _____ just _____ to Florida.

j) The prime minister's popularity (grow) _____ by 20%.

k) She (forgive/not) _____ me for not being present in the graduation ceremony.

l) I (get) _____ together with some classmates to play beach volleyball.

m) Edward (give) _____ me a strange look.

n) (go) _____ they _____ to the movies again?

o) The number of passengers (grow) _____ ten times since then.

Now check your answers by looking at the *Key to Exercises*.

UNIT 8
HANG/HAVE/HEAR/HIDE/HIT

32. HANG HUNG HUNG

PAY ATTENTION!
READ CAREFULLY THE FOLLOWING SENTENCES IN THE PAST SIMPLE.

Patrick **hung** the picture in the hall.
Rosana **hung** the calendar by the window.
Denzel **hung** the portrait next to the mirror.
Alex **hung** the overcoat behind the door.
We **hung** the paintings in the corridor.

PAY ATTENTION!
READ CAREFULLY THE FOLLOWING SENTENCES IN THE PRESENT PERFECT TENSE.

He **has hung** the sweater in the wardrobe.
Emma **hasn't hung** out the laundry yet.
My aunt **has** just **hung** the towels on the washing line.
I **have hung** around all day long waiting for your phone call.
Definetely Arthur is not polite. He **has** just **hung** up on me!

NOTE

**HANG IS A REGULAR VERB WHEN IT MEANS DEATH BY HANGING.
THEY HANGED HIM FOR MURDER.**

33. HAVE HAD HAD

PAY ATTENTION!
READ CAREFULLY THE FOLLOWING SENTENCES IN THE PAST SIMPLE.

Jane **had** a beauty salon when she lived in Montreal.
Leslie and I **had** a great time while we were in Hawaii.
They **had** a short conversation about their hobbies.
I **had** only 10 minutes to take a shower.
The art gallery **had** many visitors last weekend.

PAY ATTENTION!
READ CAREFULLY THE FOLLOWING SENTENCES IN THE PRESENT PERFECT SIMPLE.

As usual Martha **has had** a bright idea!
We **haven't had** any news of Liz since she moved to Turkey.
Yuri and I **have had** a good journey.
Unfortunately they **have** already **had** an argument.
Stan **has** just **had** a chat with me.

34. HEAR HEARD HEARD

PAY ATTENTION!
READ CAREFULLY THE FOLLOWING SENTENCES IN THE PAST SIMPLE.

Bary **heard** a crash and stood up.
Bianca **heard** a strange noise about forty minutes ago.
Monica **heard** Tim and Daniel talking about ecology.
I **heard** Harry go downstairs.
We **heard** Helen might leave hospital next week.

PAY ATTENTION!
READ CAREFULLY THE FOLLOWING SENTENCES IN THE PRESENT PERFECT SIMPLE.

Have you **heard** what happened to Jimmy?
I've heard a rumour that they are lovers.
Has Gretel **heard** about the decision?
She **has** never **heard** of Mick Jagger!
Gary and I **have heard** the greatest love songs of the 1970s.

35. HIDE HID HIDDEN

PAY ATTENTION!
READ CAREFULLY THE FOLLOWING SENTENCES IN THE PAST SIMPLE.

I **hid** the photographs in the bottom drawer.
My son **hid** under my bed.
I **hid** Malcom in my cottage at the beginning of May.
Cynthia **hid** the long hair underneath the helmet.
Kenneth **hid** Anderson's present in the guest room.

PAY ATTENTION!
READ CAREFULLY THE FOLLOWING SENTENCES IN THE PRESENT PERFECT SIMPLE.

Dustin **has hidden** the documents from the investigators.
Shirley **has hidden** the fact that she was married.
I wonder why they **have hidden** everything from us in the past few weeks.
Lily **has hidden** the face in her hands.
Joy **has hidden** the black eye by wearing sunglasses.

36. HIT HIT HIT

> **PAY ATTENTION!**
> READ CAREFULLY THE FOLLOWING SENTENCES IN THE PAST SIMPLE.

The hurricane **hit** the Caribbean island at the end of 2005.

The storm **hit** Glasgow two weeks ago.

The revolutionary treatment for the disease **hit** the headlines in the early 1980s.

Miss Keller **hit** the robber with her umbrella.

Mark **hit** the head getting out of the taxi.

> **PAY ATTENTION!**
> READ CAREFULLY THE FOLLOWING SENTENCES IN THE PRESENT PERFECT SIMPLE.

The bullet **has hit** the demonstrator in the arm.

The two boxers **have hit** each other angrily.

The boat **has** just **hit** an iceberg!

The car **has hit** my dog.

Sales **have hit** a peak again.

PRACTICE MAKES PERFECT

8.1 Complete the sentences with the simple past simple of the verbs in the box. Use each verb twice.

HANG	HAVE	HEAR	HIDE	HIT

a) Marlene _____ the time of her life in Dubai.

b) Gloria _____ Rodrigo from his enemies.

c) The ball _____ my back when the kids were playing football.

d) Jessica and I _____ out together when we were at college.

e) I came into home as soon as I _____ a thunder.

f) The crystal chandelier _____ from the ceiling.

g) Joy _____ the jackpot in the beauty contest.

h) We _____ some fun while we watched the series *Friends*.

i) I put a smile on my face and _____ my sadness.

j) I _____ them celebrating the victory cheerfully.

8.2 Turn these sentences into the interrogative form.

a) They hung out last Saturday night.

_____?

b) Hilton had a Lamborghini many years ago.

_____?

c) Michelle heard them go out.

_____?

d) Martin hid evidence from the members of the jury.

_____?

e) He hit the ball as hard as he could.

_____?

8.3 Turn these sentences into the negative form.

a) Catherine hung the sun hat on the hook.

_____

b) The couple had three children.

_____

c) We heard Meg's voice.

_____

d) Stephanie hid the coupons under the pillow.

_____

e) Prices hit rock bottom.

_____

Now check your answers by looking at the *Key to Exercises*.

8.4 Complete the sentences with the present perfect simple of the verbs in brackets.

a) I (hang) _____ my tuxedo on a hanger.

b) Our country (have/not) _____ a great president over the last two decades.

c) She (hear/not) _____ of such a jewish tradition.

d) (hide) _____ the criminals _____ the body in a park?

e) My parents (hit) _____ never _____ me.

f) Tom (hang) _____ a poster on the noticeboard.

g) Paula (have/not) _____ time to see her closest friends.

h) Theresa (hear) _____ about Gil's resignation as student council president.

i) (hide) _____ Vladimir _____ anything in the library?

j) Unemployment (hit) _____ thousands of workers since the factory closed down.

k) Madeleine (hang) _____ the pink blouse in the closet.

l) I (have) _____ a tasty supper.

m) I (hear) _____ them complaining about the cost of living.

n) Jeniffer (hide) _____ euros and pounds under the rug.

o) The end of the marriage (hit) _____ Patricia hard.

Now check your answers by looking at the Key to Exercises.

UNIT 9
HOLD/HURT/KEEP/ KNOW/LEAVE

37. HOLD HELD HELD

PAY ATTENTION!
READ CAREFULLY THE FOLLOWING SENTENCES IN THE PAST SIMPLE.

In May, the prime minister **held** talks with the main opposition leaders.

I **held** Magda's shopping bags while she paid the cashier.

They **held** their hands and kissed each other.

The criminal **held** a gun in one hand.

Janice **held** the two puppies in her arms.

PAY ATTENTION!
READ CAREFULLY THE FOLLOWING SENTENCES IN THE PRESENT PERFECT SIMPLE.

I wonder why the press **has held** back information about the president's health.

The two girls **have held** a flag.

The hotel **has** just **held** our reservation.

Warren **has held** the trophy proudly.

Oprah was heartbroken, but she **has held** back the tears.

38. HURT HURT HURT

PAY ATTENTION!
READ CAREFULLY THE FOLLOWING SENTENCES IN THE PAST SIMPLE.

You **hurt** me when you said such horrible words!
I'm afraid you **hurt** Lara's feelings by telling the truth.
I don't know what really **hurt** her.
On Friday she was taken to the emergency room because her chest **hurt** a lot.
My neck **hurt** when I tried to move it.

PAY ATTENTION!
READ CAREFULLY THE FOLLOWING SENTENCES IN THE PRESENT PERFECT SIMPLE.

Has Cary **hurt** the knees in the gym?
Your criticisms **have hurt** me.
Luckily the explosion **hasn't hurt** anyone.
Ingrid fell and **has hurt** herself.
The recession **has hurt** the company's position in the market.

39. KEEP KEPT KEPT

PAY ATTENTION!
READ THE FOLLOWING SENTENCES IN THE PAST SIMPLE.

Sabrina **kept** looking at me while I was talking to Tina.
Somebody **kept** ringing the doorbell.
I **kept** my eyes closed for forty minutes.
Ron **kept** interrupting me all the time.
Witney **kept** fit by walking two miles every single day.

PAY ATTENTION!
READ THE FOLLOWING SENTENCES IN THE PRESENT PERFECT SIMPLE.

They **haven't kept** their homes clean.
I **have kept** the children busy for 2 hours.
She **hasn't kept** her house tidy during the week.
Hermann **has kept** his father's diary for years.
David **has kept** us in suspense for two weeks.

40. KNOW KNEW KNOWN

PAY ATTENTION!
READ CAREFULLY THE FOLLOWING SENTENCES IN THE PAST SIMPLE.

Rita **knew** everything about Robson's intentions when they travelled together to Morocco.
I'm sure Angelina **knew** nothing about skateboarding.
I **knew** he wouldn't take my advice.
Gabriel **knew** about the effects of smoking on the body.
Sue **knew** the details of the story inside out.

PAY ATTENTION!
READ CAREFULLY THE FOLLOWING SENTENCES IN THE PRESENT PERFECT SIMPLE.

Marlon and I **have known** each other for a long time.
I **have known** about your secret life since last year.
How long **has** she **known** Gregory?
Walter **has known** my brother since they were in the army together.
I **have known** from experience that this kind of strategy doesn't work.

41. LEAVE LEFT LEFT

> **PAY ATTENTION!**
> READ CAREFULLY THE FOLLOWING SENTENCES IN THE PAST SIMPLE.

The plane **left** Lisbon two hours ago.

My girlfriend **left** for work in the early morning.

I **left** home when I was 19.

Virginia **left** the country last year because she got a job in Ireland.

The biography **left out** key aspects of John Kennedy's life.

> **PAY ATTENTION!**
> READ CAREFULLY THE FOLLOWING SENTENCES IN THE PRESENT PERFECT SIMPLE.

Francis **has** just **left** Sidney for Melbourne.

George is so absent-minded. He **has left** the lights on again!

Marcia **has left** the company lately.

Have you **left** your wallet at home?

Sandie **has left** behind a few belongings.

PRACTICE MAKES PERFECT

9.1 Complete the sentences with the past simple form of the verbs in the box. Use each verb twice.

| HOLD | HURT | KEEP | KNOW | LEAVE |

a) Timothy _____ back his comments about your attitude.

b) Josef _____ little about the side effects of the treatment.

c) Erick and Mick _____ themselves climbing the wall.

d) Tom _____ home early today.

e) Trevor was upset but _____ the sense of humour.

f) Monika _____ onto the handrail while she went up the first flight of stairs.

g) Your stupid words _____ me profoundly.

h) Gunter _____ all the promises he made.

i) No one _____ how hard the journey would be.

j) Diana _____ Barcelona at nine in the morning.

9.2 Turn these sentences into the interrogative form.

a) They held a reception to welcome the British ambassador.
_____?

b) Keanu hurt his arm playing handball.
_____?

c) Francine kept up with her studies.
_____?

d) Sonia knew the risks of the surgery.
_____?

e) The bus left the station fifteen minutes late.
_____?

9.3 Turn these sentences into the negative form.

a) The National Museum held an exhibition of Salvador Dali's work in January.
_____.

b) It hurt me to hear Liz was insensitive about the matter.
_____.

c) Louise kept herself out of trouble.
_____.

d) Joseph knew Peter was a talented architect.
_____.

e) Martin left work at 6.15 p.m.
_____.

Now check your answers by looking at the *Key to Exercises*.

9.4 Complete the sentences with the present perfect simple of the verbs in brackets.

a) The Secretary of Defense (hold) _____ the post for 3 years.

b) I (hurt) _____ myself with the pocket knife.

c) Mr. Gates (keep) _____ the conversation going.

d) How long (know) _____ you _____ my parents?

e) George (leave) _____ everyone waiting for two hours!

f) They (hold) _____ the convention at the most sophisticated hotel in town.

g) Claire tripped over the toys and (hurt) _____ her elbow.

h) (keep) _____ the artists _____ your attention?

i) I (know) _____ Guy's father for 7 years.

j) Christine (leave) _____ her partner of 12 years for a younger man.

k) Judy and I wanted to laugh, but we (hold) _____ ourselves back.

l) (hurt) _____ Tim _____ the ankle?

m) My wife and I (keep) _____ the kids off junk food.

n) I (Know) _____ about Gary's plans since March.

o) Frank (leave) _____ Canada to live in Spain.

Now check your answers by looking at the *Key to Exercises*.

UNIT 10
LEND/LET/LIE/LIGHT/LOSE

42. LEND LENT LENT

PAY ATTENTION!
READ CAREFULLY THE FOLLOWING SENTENCES IN THE PAST SIMPLE.

Dinah **lent** me $200 until Friday.

Michael **lent** me some tools so that I could fix the vacuum cleaner.

My neighbour **lent** me a ladder three days ago.

Jean **lent** me a big backpack.

I **lent** George $300, but he has never paid me back.

PAY ATTENTION!
READ CAREFULLY THE FOLLOWING SENTENCES IN THE PRESENT PERFECT SIMPLE.

Phill **has lent me** an English-French dictionary.

I **have lent** Karen a pair of gloves that I bought in Milan.

Patrick **hasn't lent me** the lawnmower.

David **has lent** me two thousand euros.

I **have** just **lent** Paul my bicycle.

43. LET LET LET

PAY ATTENTION!
READ CAREFULLY THE FOLLOWING SENTENCES IN THE PAST SIMPLE.

She **let** the kids do whatever they liked.
I **let** the kids swim for 2 hours.
Last month the teacher **let** some students take the test again.
Liz **let** Mrs. Peck in and sent her to the marketing department.
Of course I **let** Shelley talk about herself, but she kept quiet.

PAY ATTENTION!
READ CAREFULLY THE FOLLOWING SENTENCES IN THE PRESENT PERFECT SIMPLE.

Greg **has let** the windows open.
The last concerts **have let** down the majority of her fans.
Dad **has let** me go out.
Barry **has let** his daughter drive from San Francisco to San Diego.
The Scotland Yard inspectors **haven't let** them leave the country.

44. LIE LAY LAIN

PAY ATTENTION!
READ CAREFULLY THE FOLLOWING SENTENCES IN THE PAST SIMPLE.

Helga **lay down** on the bed and started reading *Crime and Punishment*.
Mia **lay down** on the grass and looked at the stars.
Woody and I **lay** flat on the floor to do the next exercise.
Irene **lay** down on the couch and turned on the TV.
I **lay** back in the chair and thought of Giovanna.

PAY ATTENTION!
READ CAREFULLY THE FOLLOWING SENTENCES IN THE PRESENT PERFECT SIMPLE.

Vivian **has lain** in the sun.
Gregory **has** just **lain** down to have a good rest.
Ivan **has lain** back and has laughed.
The equipment **has lain** idle for ages.
The dog **has lain** in the patio for hours.

 **NOTE**

**LIE IS A REGULAR VERB WHEN IT MEANS "SAY SOMETHING WHICH IS NOT TRUE".
HE LIED ABOUT HIS AGE.**

45. LIGHT LIT LIT

PAY ATTENTION!
READ CAREFULLY THE FOLLOWING SENTENCES IN THE PAST SIMPLE.

Daisy **lit** the fire and phoned Jim.

Everyone looked at Rod when he **lit** a cigarette.

We **lit** the way by carrying some torches.

They **lit** up the fountain.

My eyes **lit** up with satisfaction.

PAY ATTENTION!
READ CAREFULLY THE FOLLOWING SENTENCES IN THE PRESENT PERFECT SIMPLE.

Andressa **has** just **lit** the candles.

The moon **has lit** the night.

The fireworks **have lit** up the sky.

Kevin **has lit** the grill.

As expected, Andy's face **has lit** up with enthusiasm.

46. LOSE LOST LOST

> **PAY ATTENTION!**
> READ CAREFULLY THE FOLLOWING SENTENCES IN THE PAST SIMPLE.

I **lost** my appetite when I heard Vincent had been fired.

Anthony **lost** his best friend in a plane crash.

Max **lost** interest in soccer in his teens.

Ingrid **lost** the brooch when she was in the convenience store.

When she **lost** her job, the future looked completely uncertain.

> **PAY ATTENTION!**
> READ CAREFULLY THE FOLLOWING SENTENCES IN THE PRESENT PERFECT SIMPLE.

It's hard to believe that Mercedez **has lost** the diamond ring!

She **has lost** her mother lately.

Charlton is on a diet and **has lost** weight during the past few weeks.

Have you **lost** confidence in your assistant?

Have you ever **lost** your identity card?

PRACTICE MAKES PERFECT

10.1 Complete the sentences with the past simple of the verbs below. Use each verb twice.

| LEND | LET | LIE | LIGHT | LOSE |

a) Now Christine stays focused on the present.
She _____ the past go.

b) Mom _____ the birthday candle and everybody sang *Happy Birthday*.

c) I _____ Frank a black shirt.

d) The aircraft _____ altitude.

e) William _____ down on the bed and cried.

f) Lucy's parents _____ her come with me.

g) Patrick _____ his balance and fell.

h) I _____ her a grammar book, but she didn't give it back.

i) Arthur _____ on the ground and stared at the rainbow.

j) The flashlight _____ the path to the hut.

10.2 Turn these sentences into the interrogative form.

a) The bank lent the company a great deal of money.
_____?

b) They let Gregory decide what to do.
_____?

c) Liz lay down for a while on the sofa.
_____?

d) Ivan lit the campfire.
_____?

e) Boris lost the sight in one eye.
_____?

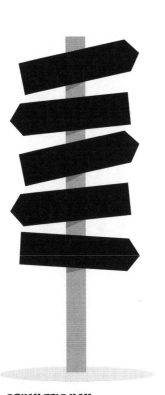

10.3 Turn these sentences into the negative form.

a) Neil lent Paul a notepad.

    _____.

b) I let them eat fatty food.

    _____.

c) Deryl lay back in the chair.

    _____.

d) They lit up the statue.

    _____.

e) The clerk lost his temper with the stubborn customer.

    _____.

Now check your answers looking at the *Key to Exercises*.

10.4 Complete the sentences with the present perfect simple of the verbs in brackets.

a) Terry (lend) _____ support to the agreement.

b) Gregory (let) _____ the property fall to pieces.

c) I (lie) _____ on my back.

d) Mandy (light/not) _____ the cigar.

e) (lose) _____ she _____ the baby?

f) She (lend) _____ me a hand with the lesson planning.

g) (let) _____ you _____ them eat candies?

h) Don't disturb Renee! He (lie) _____ just _____ down.

i) The lightning (light) _____ up the dark ranch.

j) (lose) _____ you _____ hope for a better world?

k) Lara (lose) _____ touch with Ken since he moved to Singapore.

l) Sophia (let) _____ her dog out.

m) The house (lie) _____ empty for two years.

n) The pretty top models (light) _____ up the fashion show.

o) The famous actress (lend) _____ her name to an international charity.

Now check your answers by looking at the Key to Exercises.

UNIT 11
MAKE/MEAN/MEET/PAY/PUT

47. MAKE MADE MADE

PAY ATTENTION!
READ CAREFULLY THE FOLLOWING SENTENCES IN THE PAST SIMPLE.

I **made** a shopping list of all the things I want you to buy.
Morgan **made** an incredible effort to help us.
Doris **made** friends with a young doctor last year.
We **made** some sandwiches for the picnic.
Axel **made** a funny suggestion but none of us laughed.

PAY ATTENTION!
READ CAREFULLY THE FOLLOWING SENTENCES IN THE PRESENT PERFECT SIMPLE.

The glass **has made** a mark on my desk.
You **have** just **made** the most important decision of your life.
Have you **made** the chocolate cake yet?
I **have** already **made** breakfast.
The Swiss airline **has made** huge profits lately.

48. MEAN MEANT MEANT

> **PAY ATTENTION!**
> READ CAREFULLY THE FOLLOWING SENTENCES IN THE PAST SIMPLE.

I'm sure she **meant** to upset you.
Bruce **meant** what he said yesterday evening.
Ursula showed the old piece of jewellery but it **meant** nothing to us.
Being a pianist **meant** the world to Baden.
The truckers' strike **meant** trouble to the entire population.

> **PAY ATTENTION!**
> READ CAREFULLY THE FOLLOWING SENTENCES IN THE PRESENT PERFECT SIMPLE.

There's no doubt my gesture of goodwill **has meant** something to Markus.
Such achievements **have meant** you have a promising career as a businessman.
You'll never know how much our relationship **has meant** to me.
Your recognition of our competence **has meant** so much to the team!
These figures **have meant** we're doing well financially speaking.

49. MEET MET MET

PAY ATTENTION!
READ CAREFULLY THE FOLLOWING SENTENCES IN THE PAST SIMPLE.

They first **met** in Venice in 1997.
I **met** an old school friend when I went shopping yesterday.
We **met** each other in front of the opera house.
He **met** his wife at university.
Glynn **met** us at the airport.

PAY ATTENTION!
READ CAREFULLY THE FOLLOWING SENTENCES IN THE PRESENT PERFECT SIMPLE.

Have you ever **met** a celebrity?
I **have** just **met** a very interesting person.
Diana **has** already **met** all her clients this week.
They **haven't met** each other until now.
Dante **has met** a pretty girl in the hostel.

50. PAY PAID PAID

PAY ATTENTION!
READ CAREFULLY THE FOLLOWING SENTENCES IN THE PAST SIMPLE.

Last year my father **paid** for my singing classes.
Tim **paid** the gas bill yesterday.
Tracey **paid** three workmen to repair her house.
I'm sure I **paid** in cash.
Eva **paid** them back two days ago.

PAY ATTENTION!
READ CAREFULLY THE FOLLOWING SENTENCES IN THE PRESENT PERFECT SIMPLE.

The cruel dictator **has paid** for his crimes.
Mr. Hopkins **has** already **paid** his debts.
You **haven't paid** attention to the warning!
John **has paid** seventy dollars for the two books.
Have you **paid** for your groceries?

51. PUT PUT PUT

> **PAY ATTENTION!**
> READ CAREFULLY THE FOLLOWING SENTENCES IN THE PAST SIMPLE.

Jodie **put** the two catologues in the cabinet.

There was peace because we **put** aside our differences.

I **put** my name at the top of the page.

Janet **put** the proposal at the beginning of the meeting.

They **put** on their new running shoes.

> **PAY ATTENTION!**
> READ CAREFULLY THE FOLLOWING SENTENCES IN THE PRESENT PERFECT SIMPLE.

They **have put off** the match because of the bad weather.

Carol **has put** on a lot of weight over the last weeks.

I **have put** my hand up to ask about the causes of the Wall Street Crash of 1929.

Ronald **hasn't put** his plans into action yet.

Where **has** she **put** my appointment book?

PRACTICE MAKES PERFECT

11.1 Complete the sentences with the past simple of the verbs in the box. Use each verb twice.

| MAKE | MEAN | MEET | PAY | PUT |

a) We _____ each other at the Woodstock Festival in 1969.

b) Katie's hairdo _____ her look younger.

c) Getting an email from Kim _____ my day.

d) Karl _____ for my psychotherapy sessions.

e) Helen _____ some food in her mouth.

f) Such indifference _____ they didn't care about us.

g) The boss _____ all the employees in cash.

h) The grades _____ Al was a terrific student.

i) Hillary _____ an old friend of hers in the Frankfurt Book Fair.

j) The speaker _____ into words how many citizens felt.

11.2 Turn these sentences into the interrogative form.

a) Ryan made the most of the weekend in the campsite.

_____?

b) Your commitment meant better days for all them.

_____?

c) They met tourists from all over the world last summer.

_____?

d) Walt paid the tablet by credit card.

_____?

e) Raissa put the kids to bed around eleven o'clock.

_____?

11.3 Turn these sentences into the negative form.

a) Glenda made a fuss about the parking fine.

   _____.

b) Melania meant to cheat you.

   _____.

c) Susan and Sidney met at college.

   _____.

d) They paid a visit to the medieval cathedral.

   _____.

e) Emily put herself in an embarassing situation.

   _____.

Now check your answers looking at the *Key to Exercises*.

11.4 Complete the sentences with the present perfect simple of the verbs in brackets.

a) Politics (mean) _____ nothing to Nick in the past years.

b) Your expertise (mean/not) _____ a positive working environment for all of us.

c) I (meet) _____ Sam in Harrods Street.

d) (pay) _____ she _____ a fine for speeding?

e) They(put) _____ the theory into practice.

f) Joy (make) _____ up Wendel as a clown.

g) I don't know what Gunter (mean) _____ by *elusive*.

h) Andrew and I (meet) _____ already _____ one another many times.

i) The tourists (pay) _____ for the trip six weeks in advance.

j) Your reaction (put) _____ our lives in danger.

k) That dress (make) _____ Carol feel fat.

l) Rike and Randal (make) _____ up a poor excuse.

m) (meet) _____ the German prime minister _____ the American president?

n) We (pay/not) _____ them back yet.

o) (put) _____ you _____ the brochure in your briefcase?

Now check your answers by looking at the *Key to Exercises*.

UNIT 12
READ/RIDE/RING/RISE/RUN

52. READ READ READ

> **PAY ATTENTION!**
> READ CAREFULLY THE FOLLOWING SENTENCES IN THE PAST SIMPLE.

When I **read** between the lines, everything became clear.

Nancy **read** the script as if nothing was going on around her.

Krystal **read** aloud the lyrics of the song.

I **read** my e-mails while she updated the blog.

Serena's grandmother **read** fairy tales to her when she was very young.

> **PAY ATTENTION!**
> READ CAREFULLY THE FOLLOWING SENTENCES IN THE PRESENT PERFECT SIMPLE.

They **have** never **read** about the Cold War before.

Diego **has read** *Pride and Prejudice* by Jane Austen.

Have you ever **read** *War and Peace* ?

It looks like Daniel **has read** my mind.

Mia **has read** the step-by-step instructions carefully to switch on the machine.

 **NOTE**

READ IS PRONOUNCED RED IN THE PAST SIMPLE AND PAST PARTICIPLE FORMS.

53. RIDE RODE RIDDEN

PAY ATTENTION!
READ CAREFULLY THE FOLLOWING SENTENCES IN THE PAST SIMPLE.

The boat **road** the waves.
Valerie **rode** through the fields.
Shirley **rode** the bus to school two hours ago.
The kids and I **rode** in the back seat.
The couple **rode** the train from Glasgow to Cambridge.

PAY ATTENTION!
READ CAREFULLY THE FOLLOWING SENTENCES IN THE PRESENT PERFECT SIMPLE.

Debora **has** never **ridden** a bicycle.
Juan says that he **has** already **ridden** a bull.
Alice **has ridden** the elevator to the top floor.
Gabriel **has ridden** on the surfboard and has enjoyed himself for hours.
Have you ever **ridden** a roller coaster?

54. RING RANG RUNG

> **PAY ATTENTION!**
> READ CAREFULLY THE FOLLOWING SENTENCES IN THE PAST SIMPLE.

I **rang** for the butler but he didn't appear.
As soon as the fire started, the alarm **rang**.
Ramona was having a bath when the phone **rang.**
Christina **rang** me to let me know she was fine.
I **rang** the clinic to make an appointment with Dr. Peltier.

> **PAY ATTENTION!**
> READ CAREFULLY THE FOLLOWING SENTENCES IN THE PRESENT PERFECT SIMPLE.

I **have rung** the doorbell four times.
She **hasn't rung** me because she doesn't have my number.
Fred and Flora **have rung** and they want you to ring them back.
Brendon **has** just **rung** for a cab.
I **haven't rung** my fiancée yet.

55. RISE ROSE RISEN

PAY ATTENTION!
READ CAREFULLY THE FOLLOWING SENTENCES IN THE PAST SIMPLE.

Fiona became nervous and her voice **rose**.
They **rose** in rebellion against the emperor.
The patient's temperature **rose,** so he took his medicine.
Inflation **rose** by 5% last month.
Vladimir Putin **rose** to power in 2000.

PAY ATTENTION!
READ CAREFULLY THE FOLLOWING SENTENCES IN THE PRESENT PERFECT SIMPLE.

Sales **have risen** by 40% so far.
The balloon **has risen** to the porch ceiling.
Crime rates **haven't risen** in Miami since 2010.
The price of petrol **has risen** again!
The sun **has** already **risen.**

 **NOTE**

DON'T CONFUSE RISE AND RAISE.
RAISE IS A REGULAR VERB: RAISE/ RAISED / RAISED.
I RAISED MY HAND BECAUSE I KNEW THE ANSWER.

56. RUN RAN RUN

> **PAY ATTENTION!**
> READ CAREFULLY THE FOLLOWING SENTENCES IN THE PAST SIMPLE.

Louis **ran** fast to catch the bus.

Leo **ran** a real estate agency in Houston two years ago.

The famous athlete **ran** a terrific race.

They **ran** as fast as they could.

Laura **ran** screaming, trying to get some kind of help.

> **PAY ATTENTION!**
> READ CAREFULLY THE FOLLOWING SENTENCES IN THE PRESENT PERFECT SIMPLE.

Catherine **has run** to the seaport.

It's the second time Claire **has run** away from home.

Have you ever **run** a marathon?

The little girl started laughing and **has run** to her mother.

She **hasn't run** her own business yet because she's very insecure.

PRACTICE MAKES PERFECT

12.1 Complete the sentences with the past simple of the verbs in the box below. Use each verb twice.

| READ | RIDE | RING | RISE | RUN |

a) Humphrey _____ a camel in the Sahara desert.

b) I _____ to the top of my career and became a well respected CEO.

c) Charlotte _____ the text attentively.

d) Mel and I _____ a mile in ten minutes.

e) The alarm clock _____ at 4.45 a.m.

f) Gabriel _____ a passage from the Bible.

g) The small child _____ on my shoulders.

h) Joseph Stalin _____ to power in 1930.

i) Andrei was in danger and _____ for his life.

j) Gloria was out when I _____ her back.

12.2 Turn these sentences into the interrogative form.

a) Joyce read a report about climate change.
   _____?

b) Carrie rode the subway every day last week.
   _____?

c) Ronda rang back as soon as she found the voucher.
   _____?

d) The unemployment rate rose in many European countries at that time.
   _____?

e) They ran out of gas.
   _____?

12.3 Turn these sentences into the negative form.

a) Cindy read a short story by Jack London.
   _____.

b) The kids rode the merry-go-round.
   _____.

c) Spencer rang the company to get some information about the job.
   _____.

d) The birth rate rose last year.
   _____.

e) Naomi ran towards the gate.
   _____.

Now check your answers by looking at the *Key to Exercises*.

12.4 Complete the sentences with the present perfect simple of the verbs in brackets.

a) Denzel (read) _____ *The Name of Rose* twice.

b) Glynn (ride/not) _____ his bike on the sidewalk.

c) I (ring) _____ for the elevator.

d) Daniel's voice (rise) _____ in despair.

e) Philip (run) _____ down the street to catch the thief.

f) (read) _____ you _____ again *Alice in the Wonderland* ?

g) Bradley (ride) _____ never _____ a Ferris Wheel.

h) The phone (ring) _____ all day long.

i) (rise) _____ the sales _____ over the past months?

j) The lorry (run) _____ out of control and hit a tree.

k) Clive (read) _____ about Leonardo Messi in a French sports magazine.

l) I (ride) _____ up the escalator.

m) (ring) _____ you _____ the bell yet?

IRREGULAR VERBS: THE ULTIMATE GUIDE

n) Modern skyscrapers (rise) _____ in downtown.

o) He (run) _____ for president four times!

Now check your answers by looking the *Key to Exercises.*

UNIT 13
SAY/SEE/SELL/SEND/SET

57. SAY SAID SAID

> **PAY ATTENTION!**
> READ CAREFULLY THE FOLLOWING SENTENCES IN THE PAST SIMPLE.

'I'm so hopeful', she **said** softly.
He **said** I was absolutely right.
Daniel **said** your point of view was wrong.
Marcia **said** inspiring words that changed my day.
They **said** the company was doing well last year.

> **PAY ATTENTION!**
> READ CAREFULLY THE FOLLOWING SENTENCES IN THE PRESENT PERFECT SIMPLE.

Have you **said** anything about Mark's working life?
I **have** just **said** hello to David.
He **has said** something to Robert.
Diane **has said** Pablo is dumb and foolish.
She **has** just **said** you intend to live in Atlanta.

58. SEE SAW SEEN

PAY ATTENTION!
READ CAREFULLY THE FOLLOWING SENTENCES IN THE PAST SIMPLE.

At the time I **saw** him as a well-informed and communicative person.

She **saw** Peter take away the watches.

Last Thursday I **saw** an exclusive interview with John Travolta.

She **saw** that the sun was rising.

Hillary went into town yesterday and **saw** Andrew.

PAY ATTENTION!
READ CAREFULLY THE FOLLOWING SENTENCES IN THE PRESENT PERFECT SIMPLE.

Have you **seen** Sean?

I **have** just **seen** the job ad in the paper.

We **haven't seen** each other for years.

Have you **seen** Victor as a reliable person?

I **haven't seen** my grandchildren lately.

59. SELL SOLD SOLD

> **PAY ATTENTION!**
> READ CAREFULLY THE FOLLOWING SENTENCES IN THE PAST SIMPLE.

Henry **sold** his flat last month.

Elvis **sold** his car for $25,000.

At the time the rock band **sold** millions of records in a couple of months.

Last month I **sold** my stamp collection.

The clothes shop **sold** many T-shirts on Saturday.

> **PAY ATTENTION!**
> READ CAREFULLY THE FOLLOWING SENTENCES IN THE PRESENT PERFECT SIMPLE.

Those shoes **have sold** out quickly.

Lily **has sold** her mansion in Beverly Hills.

Have you **sold** your gold ring yet?

The book **has sold** very well.

We **have** already **sold** our country house.

60. SEND SENT SENT

PAY ATTENTION!
READ CAREFULLY THE FOLLOWING SENTENCES IN THE PAST SIMPLE.

Thor **sent** me pictures that he took in Thailand some months ago.
Omar **sent** us posters by mail.
The hospital **sent** an ambulance to Herbert's house.
Douglas **sent** his CV to five multinational companies.
She **sent** me her business card.

PAY ATTENTION!
READ CAREFULLY THE FOLLOWING SENTENCES IN THE PRESENT PERFECT SIMPLE.

The dishwasher wasn't working perfectly, so I **have sent** it back.
I **have sent** the university a letter of application.
It's mother's day and I **haven't sent** flowers to my mother yet.
The royal couple **has sent** out hundreds of wedding invitations.
Riz is worried because so far they **haven't sent** a reply.

61. SET SET SET

> **PAY ATTENTION!**
> READ CAREFULLY THE FOLLOWING SENTENCES IN THE PAST SIMPLE.

Hugh **set** ambitious goals for himself at the beginning of the year.
Bradley **set** himself up as a personal trainer.
The coordinator **set** guidelines which were hard to follow.
Gregor **set** a limit on how much he spends on food.
We **set** the price of the spring/summer clothing collections.

> **PAY ATTENTION!**
> READ CAREFULLY THE FOLLOWING SENTENCES IN THE PRESENT PERFECT SIMPLE.

The brilliant student **hasn't set** an example for his classmates as he should.
Christopher and I **have set** a new date for our trip.
Such proverbs **have set** me thinking.
The lack of money **has set** back the construction of the bridge.
Have you **set** the table yet?

PRACTICE MAKES PERFECT

13.1 Complete the sentences with the past simple of the verbs in the box below. Use each verb twice.

SAY	SEE	SELL	SEND	SET

a) The album *Thriller* _____ millions of copies in the 1980s.

b) Patricia didn't clap her hands when she _____ Gabriel's performance.

c) 'Make yourself at home', Pen_____ kindly.

d) The teenagers _____ up the tent in less than 20 minutes.

e) Watching that film again _____ me to sleep.

f) Mr. Murphy _____ the old clock back one hour.

g) Val _____ his hometown was founded in 1854.

h) I _____ them come into the building late in the evening.

i) Amy and I _____ our luxury yatch for $8,000,000.

j) I _____ Faye a birthday card by post.

IRREGULAR VERBS: THE ULTIMATE GUIDE

13.2 Turn these sentences into the interrogative form.

a) She said a prayer for the missing miners.

_____?

b) Yan saw Shirley walking around the square.

_____?

c) Eike sold his private jet.

_____?

d) They sent Scott a computer file.

_____?

e) Maryah set a trap to catch the coyote.

_____?

13.3 Turn these sentences into the negative form.

a) She said Keith would come back.

   _____.

b) Annabel saw the task as a challenge.

   _____.

c) John sold his cottage in 2015.

   _____.

d) I sent Ruy a thank-you letter.

   _____.

e) Carlo set to work to fix the computers.

   _____.

Now check your answers by looking at the *Key to Exercises*.

13.4 Complete the sentences with the present perfect simple of the verbs in brackets.

a) She (say) _____ we don't need much money to be happy.

b) I (see) _____ you and Elisa are getting on with each other.

c) The duty-free store in Dubai airport (sell) _____ many goods to Chinese travellers.

d) Giovanni (send/not) _____ me the price list.

e) Frank (set) _____ never _____ foot in Helen's house.

f) She walked to the door and (say) _____ goodbye to everyone.

g) As we (see) _____ in the documentary, people want to spend more time having fun.

h) The shopkeeper (sell) _____ the gadgets in a few minutes.

i) (send) _____ you _____ out the folders to our customers?

j) The candle (set) _____ fire to the dining room.

k) Raymond (say) _____ "Talk is cheap".

l) Leo (see) _____ the failure from a completely different angle.

m) They (sell) _____ the castle to a Mexican billionaire.

n) (send) _____ you _____ the package by post?

o) The company (set) _____ the target of investing heavily in technology.

Now check your answers by looking at the *Key to Exercises*.

UNIT 14
SHAKE/ SHINE/SHOOT/ SHOW/SHUT

62. SHAKE SHOOK SHAKEN

> **PAY ATTENTION!**
> READ CAREFULLY THE FOLLOWING SENTENCES IN THE PAST SIMPLE.

I **shook** Grace, but I couldn't wake her up.

The van **shook** as it went over a bump.

Mandin **shook** with fear while she watched such frightening scenes.

Spencer **shook** his head in shock.

The 2008 economic crisis **shook** countries all over the world.

> **PAY ATTENTION!**
> READ CAREFULLY THE FOLLOWING SENTENCES IN THE PRESENT PERFECT SIMPLE.

The baby took the toy and **has shaken** it.

The strong wind **has** just **shaken** the chestnut tree.

Donnie **has shaken** the dust out of the boxes.

Many buildings in Tokyo **have shaken** during the earthquake.

The predictions **haven't** yet **shaken** Will's optimism.

63. SHINE SHONE SHONE

PAY ATTENTION!
READ CAREFULLY THE FOLLOWING SENTENCES IN THE PAST SIMPLE.

The moon **shone** in the sky full of stars.
A bright light **shone** in front of us.
The British actors **shone** at the Venice Film Festival in 2012.
Franz **shone** when it was his turn to speak in public.
The pieces of furniture **shone** as if they were new.

PAY ATTENTION!
READ CAREFULLY THE FOLLOWING SENTENCES IN THE PRESENT PERFECT SIMPLE.

Her eyes **have shone** with happiness.
The sun **has shone** in the afternoon.
I polished the wooden chairs but they **haven't shone** as I expected.
The lobby was completely dark, so I **have shone** the flashlight.
The sapphire **has shone** in the shop window.

64. SHOOT SHOT SHOT

> **PAY ATTENTION!**
> READ CAREFULLY THE FOLLOWING SENTENCES IN THE PAST SIMPLE.

The night watchman **shot** the suspect in the back.
The soldiers **shot** to kill.
They **shot** the film in Australia.
I **shot** and scored three points.
Julia Roberts **shot** to fame in *Pretty Woman*.

> **PAY ATTENTION!**
> READ CAREFULLY THE FOLLOWING SENTENCES IN THE PRESENT PERFECT SIMPLE.

Have you ever **shot** a gun?
Have the bodyguards **shot** the criminals?
Eric **has shot** the rifle three times.
Patrick and I **have shot** some arrows, but they have missed the target.
Manfred **has shot** a quick glance at his teammate.

65. SHOW SHOWED SHOWN

PAY ATTENTION!
READ CAREFULLY THE FOLLOWING SENTENCES IN THE PAST SIMPLE.

I **showed** my parents the importance of a balanced diet.

My son **showed** me his latest tests a few minutes ago.

I **showed** her how to use the laptop properly.

Julie **showed** me an old map of the region.

Forest **showed** me precisely where the accident happened.

PAY ATTENTION!
READ CAREFULLY THE FOLLOWING SENTENCES IN THE PRESENT PERFECT SIMPLE.

Conrad **has shown** me that he is an extraordinary dancer.

The Japanese economy **has** already **shown** signs of recovery.

Gore **hasn't shown** any emotions.

Eva **hasn't shown** any interest in joining the online club.

They **have shown** great confidence in the project.

66. SHUT SHUT SHUT

> **PAY ATTENTION!**
> READ CAREFULLY THE FOLLOWING SENTENCES IN THE PAST SIMPLE.

I **shut** the drawer, but I didn't turn the key.

I **shut** my eyes and began breathing deeply.

Hillary **shut** the gate as she went out.

In the end, she **shut** up and listened to the expert advice.

Dylan **shut** his ears to my convincing arguments against smoking.

> **PAY ATTENTION!**
> READ CAREFULLY THE FOLLOWING SENTENCES IN THE PRESENT PERFECT SIMPLE.

We **have shut** the store later than usual.

It was cold, so I **have shut** the door.

I **haven't shut** the window because it's hot in here.

Have you **shut** your suitcase yet?

The secretary **has** just **shut** the portfolio.

PRACTICE MAKES PERFECT

14.1 Complete the sentences with the past simple of the verbs in the box. Use each verb twice.

| SHAKE | SHINE | SHOOT | SHOW | SHUT |

a) The American carmaker _____ down its factory in Argentina.

b) At the time I _____ him around the respected research center.

c) Veronika _____ her eyes to such European fashion trends!

d) The house _____ just as the train went past.

e) Brookie Shields _____ to stardom in *Blue Lagoon*.

f) I _____ my supervisor I was able to work in a team.

g) Franco walked into the forest and _____ the bear.

h) His voice _____ with anger.

i) The policewoman _____ the flashlight into the dark garage.

j) A ray of light _____ through the kitchen window.

14.2 Turn these sentences into the interrogative form.

a) The senator and the mayor shook hands.
   _____?

b) The stars shone brightly last night.
   _____?

c) They shot the movie in Greece.
   _____?

d) Hilton showed them how to use the database software.
   _____?

e) Andrew shut the back door.
   _____?

14.3 Turn these sentences into the negative form.

a) The ground shook violently.
   _____.

b) The street lights shone along the avenue.
   _____.

c) He shot me an angry look.
   _____.

d) Christian showed talent for writing fiction.
   _____.

e) They shut the door behind them.
   _____.

Now check your answers by looking at the *Key to Exercises*.

14.4 Complete the sentences with the present perfect simple using the verbs in brackets.

a) Randal (shake) _____ the bottle.

b) Frederick (shine) _____ at physics since an early age.

c) Hughes and I (shoot) _____ for the first place in the tournament.

d) She (show) _____ me amazing pictures of the Amazon forest.

e) Lily and Hans (shut) _____ themselves in the library to have a private conversation.

f) The tragedy (shake) _____ the whole nation.

g) The strong light (shine) _____ in my eyes.

h) The journalists (shoot) _____ a series of questions at me.

i) Helen (show) _____ much determination to recover from the disease.

j) (shoot) _____ the director _____ the sitcom in Los Angeles?

k) Elton (shake) _____ me by the shoulders.

l) I (shine) _____ the torch to light the cave.

m) She (shut) _____ just _____ all the windows.

n) Ruth (show) _____ excellent business skills since she started running a steak house.

o) Lilian (shut) _____ the door on her finger. It's hurting a lot!

Now check your answers by looking at the *Key to Exercises*.

UNIT 15
SING/SIT/SLEEP/SPEAK/SPEND

67. SING SANG SUNG

> **PAY ATTENTION!**
> READ CAREFULLY THE FOLLOWING SENTENCES IN THE PAST SIMPLE.

She **sang** so beautifully that everyone cried.
While Jim played the piano, we **sang** old songs.
The birds **sang** outside my window while I got up slowly.
Michael Jackson danced and **sang** brilliantly on the stage.
Chris **sang** while he painted the dining room.

> **PAY ATTENTION!**
> READ CAREFULLY THE FOLOWING SENTENCES IN THE PRESENT PERFECT SIMPLE.

She **hasn't sung** very well.
He **has sung** the most famous songs by Frank Sinatra.
Peter's aunt **has sung** to him for two hours.
Have you ever **sung** in front of thousands of people?
David **has sung** a few songs to cheer himself up.

68. SIT SAT SAT

PAY ATTENTION!
READ CAREFULLY THE FOLLOWING SENTENCES IN THE PAST SIMPLE.

Carly and I **sat** under the shade of a tree.
I was exhausted, so I **sat back** and took a nap.
All of us **sat down** to see the play.
I **sat** next to them.
We **sat** on the grass to meditate.

PAY ATTENTION!
READ CAREFULLY THE FOLLOWING SENTENCES IN THE PRESENT PERFECT SIMPLE.

Ludolf **has sat** down to take down my address.
The patient **has** just **sat** in the comfortable chair.
Sophia's teacher **has sat** her in the second row.
All the seats were taken, so I **haven't sat** down.
Have you **sat** on my new leather couch already?

69. SLEEP SLEPT SLEPT

> **PAY ATTENTION!**
> READ CAREFULLY THE FOLLOWING SENTENCES IN THE PAST SIMPLE.

Carrie **slept** well and got up in such a good mood!

That night we **slept** at Meg's house.

Cindy **slept** in her car.

She **slept** just two hours last night.

After the long journey, I **slept** for twelve hours.

> **PAY ATTENTION!**
> READ CAREFULLY THE FOLLOWING SENTENCES IN THE PRESENT PERFECT SIMPLE.

I **have** never **slept** in a hammock.

Betty was worried and **hasn't slept.**

Have you ever **slept** in a sleeping bag?

I **have** never **slept** in such a horrible room!

Robson and Alex **have slept** on the floor.

70. SPEAK SPOKE SPOKEN

PAY ATTENTION!
READ CAREFULLY THE FOLLOWING SENTENCES IN THE PAST SIMPLE.

She **spoke** to me last Monday.
I **spoke** up so that she could hear me.
Anderson **spoke** to me on the phone.
They **spoke** in German all the time.
Rocco **spoke** softly and smiled.

PAY ATTENTION!
READ CAREFULLY THE FOLLOWING SENTENCES IN THE PRESENT PERFECT SIMPLE.

Has she **spoken** to you about the change of plan?
We **haven't spoken** about the incident.
Your friends **have spoken** well of you.
Charles **has** just **spoken** for the students.
I **have spoken** my thoughts aloud.

71. SPEND SPENT SPENT

> **PAY ATTENTION!**
> READ CAREFULLY THE FOLLOWING SENTENCES IN THE PAST SIMPLE.

I **spent** my childhood in the United States.
Irvin **spent** the afternoon watching TV.
Roger **spent** a lot of time playing video games.
Alfred and I **spent** $10,000 on the trip to the Netherlands.
I **spent** the whole day trying to get in touch with Elizabeth.

> **PAY ATTENTION!**
> READ CAREFULLY THE FOLLOWING SENTENCES IN THE PRESENT PERFECT SIMPLE.

I **have spent** more time with my family in the recent weeks.
Have you **spent** a lot of money on shoes?
The government **hasn't spent** much money on education.
She **has** just **spent** the summer holidays in Ibiza.
Farah **has spent** $6,000 on a ruby pendant.

PRACTICE MAKES PERFECT

15.1 Complete the sentences with the past simple of the verbs below. Use each verb twice.

| SING | SIT | SLEEP | SPEAK | SPEND |

a) Christine told me she _____ like a log!

b) David was sent to prison just because he _____ his mind.

c) The fans went wild when Madonna _____ Material Girl.

d) Ted _____ much time to answer the question.

e) Fred _____ down and had a look at the notes.

f) I _____ my free time playing sports.

g) Mark _____ us a romantic Italian song.

h) My wife and I _____ in our new bed.

i) Bella _____ back and watched the kids having fun in the backyard.

j) She turned to the foreigner and _____ some words in Arabic.

15.2 Turn these sentences into the interrogative form.

a) Dad sang a song by *The Beatles*.

   _____?

b) The little girl sat down to watch cartoons.

   _____?

c) Christine slept on the sofa.

   _____?

d) They spoke about their professions.

   _____?

e) Wanderson spent a lot of money on himself.

   _____?

15.3 Turn the following sentences into the negative form.

a) Thomas sang all night long.

   _____.

b) They sat down to discuss the new policy.

   _____.

c) I slept late last Sunday.

   _____.

d) Serena spoke clearly and slowly.

   _____.

e) The previous administration spent billions of dollars on health care services.

   _____.

Now check your answers by looking at the *Key to Exercises*.

15.4 Complete the sentences in the present perfect simple using the verbs in brackets.

a) Laura (sing) _____ a song by Phill Collins.

b) Samuel (sleep) _____ never _____ outside before.

c) Sabrina (sit) _____ quietly in the front seat of the vehicle.

d) (speak) _____ you _____ to Luca and Robert about your suspicions?

e) Will (spend) _____ the days cycling and running.

f) Raul (sing) _____ as well as we thought he would.

g) Virginia (sit/not) _____ upright on the bench.

h) She (sleep/not) _____ many hours over last week.

i) So far Anderson (speak / not) _____ about what happened.

j) My wife and I (spend) _____ $50,000 to repair the house.

k) I (sing) _____ along to the radio.

l) We stopped walking and (sit) _____ around for a while.

m) Amyr went to bed early and (sleep) _____ just _____.

n) I (speak) _____ at the Arts Annual Convention.

o) Agnes (spend) _____ a long period of time in South Korea.

Now check your answers by looking at the *Key to Exercises*.

UNIT 16
STAND/ STEAL/ STRIKE/SWIM/TAKE

72. STAND STOOD STOOD

> **PAY ATTENTION!**
> READ CAREFULLY THE FOLLOWING SENTENCES IN THE PAST SIMPLE.

They **stood** for a long time in front of the palace.
I **stood** on my tiptoes to reach the top shelf.
Wenzel just **stood** there looking at me.
She **stood up** from the table and walked to the restroom.
Bradley **stood up** to introduce himself.

> **PAY ATTENTION!**
> READ CAREFULLY THE FOLLOWING SENTENCES IN THE PRESENT PERFECT SIMPLE.

Lauren **has stood** still and listened carefully to what I said.
Shakespeare's literature **has stood** the test of time.
The police officers arrived, but the crowd **hasn't stood** back.
The medieval castle **has stood** in the top of the mountain for centuries.
They gave up attacking us because we **have stood** together.

73. STEAL STOLE STOLEN

> **PAY ATTENTION!**
> READ CAREFULLY THE FOLLOWING SENTENCES IN THE PAST SIMPLE.

Two guys broke into the shop and **stole** $900 in cash.
Erickson **stole** some tulips from the florist's.
The thieves **stole** valuable works of art from the museum.
I wonder why they **stole** such documents.
I find it hard to believe that Susan **stole** my purse!

> **PAY ATTENTION!**
> READ CAREFULLY THE FOLOWING SENTENCES IN THE PRESENT PERFECT SIMPLE.

Patrick **has stolen** money from his workmates.
Edgar **has** just **stolen** my incredible idea!
Ray **has stolen** the ball four times in the second half.
Someone **has stolen** Joyce's earrings.
Thieves **have stolen** Patricia's car.

74. STRIKE STRUCK STRUCK

> **PAY ATTENTION!**
> READ CAREFULLY THE FOLLOWING SENTENCES IN THE PAST SIMPLE.

Gary **struck** the arm against the wall.

The word *infidelity* **struck** fear into Ben's heart.

Spencer **struck** a match and set fire to the old pamphlets.

Eventually Grace and I **struck** a balance between our personal and professional lives.

Gina **struck** a pose and smiled broadly.

> **PAY ATTENTION!**
> READ CAREFULLY THE FOLLOWING SENTENCES IN THE PRESENT PERFECT SIMPLE.

The shocking reports **have struck** a blow against the president's image.

The two countries **have struck** a deal to attract more investments in the long term.

The living room clock **has struck** 10:15 p.m.

Celine was heavily criticised but she **hasn't struck** back.

A disturbing thought **has struck** Noel.

75. SWIM SWAM SWUM

PAY ATTENTION!
READ CAREFULLY THE FOLLOWING SENTENCES IN THE PAST SIMPLE.

The American swimmer Gertrude Ederle **swam** across the English Channel in 1926.
He **swam** across the Volga River.
The dolphins **swam** next to the ferry.
I **swam** in the mornings to relax my mind and body.
Madeleine **swam** every day to qualify for the championship.

PAY ATTENTION!
READ CAREFULLY THE FOLLLOWING SENTENCES IN THE PRESENT PERFECT SIMPLE.

The whales **have swum** in the clear blue waters.
I **haven't swum** for years.
The water was cold, so Darren **hasn't swum**.
The kids **have** already **swum** today.
Jacqueline **has swum** from one end of the pool to the other.

IRREGULAR VERBS: THE ULTIMATE GUIDE

76. TAKE TOOK TAKEN

> **PAY ATTENTION!**
> **READ CAREFULLY THE FOLLOWING SENTENCES IN THE PAST SIMPLE.**

I **took** a look at the illustrations you made. They are amazing!

Steve Jobs **took** interest in Buddhism when he was nineteen years old.

The two brothers **took** their relatives to the train station.

Because it was hot, Beryl **took** off the coat.

I'm sure Randolph **took** pride in his work.

> **PAY ATTENTION!**
> **READ CAREFULLY THE FOLLOWING SENTENCES IN THE PRESENT PERFECT SIMPLE.**

Marcel **has** just **taken** a shower.

Liz **has taken** a pen from my pencil case.

Nobody knows why she **hasn't taken** the job.

The plane **has** just **taken** off.

We **have taken** many photographs of Niagara Falls.

PRACTICE MAKES PERFECT

16.1 Complete the sentences with the past simple of the verbs in the box. Use each verb twice.

| STAND | STEAL | STRIKE | SWIM | TAKE |

a) Jeff _____ in line for 40 minutes.

b) The shoplifter _____ some trousers from the outlet store.

c) Steven _____ across the lake.

d) My father _____ me to a ski resort when I was twelve years old.

e) I _____ up a friendship with a flight attendant.

f) Lightning _____ the farmhouse.

g) The ducks _____ around the pond.

h) Hannah and Santiago _____ watching the snow fall.

i) As soon as we saw the animals in their natural habitat, we _____ lots of pictures.

j) It looks as if Marcello _____ your sister's heart.

IRREGULAR VERBS: THE ULTIMATE GUIDE

16.2 Turn these sentences into the interrogative form.

a) Frank stood out in the job market.
   _____?

b) Rick stole the scene again.
   _____?

c) The SUV struck a lorry.
   _____?

d) She swam in the Pacific Ocean.
   _____?

e) They took your experience into account.
   _____?

16.3 Turn these sentences into the negative form.

a) Marcia stood close to the huge tree.

   _____.

b) The thieves stole computers and TV sets.

   _____.

c) The boat struck a large rock.

   _____.

d) Sonia swam every single day when she lived by the sea.

   _____.

e) Gordon took care of the children when his wife was away.

   _____.

Now check your answers by looking at the *Key to Exercises*.

16.4 Complete the sentences in the present perfect simple using the verbs in brackets.

a) I (stand) _____ up to close the curtains.

b) Alfred (steal) _____ the show with a superb tap dancing performance.

c) Finally the young miners (strike) _____ gold!

d) (swim) _____ you ever _____ in a river?

e) I wonder why they (take/not) _____ me seriously.

f) He (stand) _____ up straight to do the stretching exercise.

g) Someone (steal) _____ my bike!

h) Lily fell and (strike) _____ the face against the ground.

i) Tina and Albert (swim) _____ in the warm water.

j) It (take) _____ me so long to find the tie I was looking for.

k) She (stand) _____ there looking at the street performers.

l) (steal) _____ they _____ your money?

m) The stone (strike) _____ Sean on the nose.

n) Billie (swim) _____ incredibly well. It's the first time he has got a medal!

o) I (take) _____ down everything you said in the lecture.

Now check your answers by looking at the *Key to Exercises*.

UNIT 17
TEACH/TEAR/TELL/THINK/THROW

77. TEACH TAUGHT TAUGHT

PAY ATTENTION!
READ CAREFULLY THE FOLLOWING SENTENCES IN THE PAST SIMPLE.

I **taught** Courtney to play tennis when she was a teenager.
My sister **taught** biology at a private school.
My mother **taught** me to drive.
Glen **taught** at London University in the 1980s.
She **taught** me everything I know about running a travel agency.

PAY ATTENTION!
READ CAREFULLY THE FOLLOWING SENTENCES IN THE PRESENT PERFECT SIMPLE.

I **have** already **taught** English to French students.
My parents **have taught** me the importance of good manners.
Mr. Barron **has taught** American literature at the University of California.
My grandfather **has taught** me the art of storytelling.
Max is a great swimmer but he **hasn't taught** his kids to swim.

78. TEAR TORE TORN

> **PAY ATTENTION!**
> READ CAREFULLY THE FOLLOWING SENTENCES IN THE PAST SIMPLE.

Terence **tore** the newspaper furiously.
The table cloth **tore** just as I pulled it.
Noelly **tore** up the silk sheet.
Cindy **tore** the dress as she was coming up the stairs.
Vivian **tore** the skirt while she was washing it.

> **PAY ATTENTION!**
> READ CAREFULLY THE FOLLOWING SENTENCES IN THE PRESENT PERFECT SIMPLE.

I **have** just **torn** my shirt on a nail.
Meg **has torn** the recipes to pieces.
The argument **has torn** us apart.
Humphrey **has torn** all the envelopes that Maurice kept.
Witney **has torn** her blouse again!

79. TELL TOLD TOLD

PAY ATTENTION!
READ CAREFULLY THE FOLLOWING SENTENCES IN THE PAST SIMPLE.

Mr. Spears **told** everyone your secret!
I **told** them to be quiet.
Sebastian **told** us that the geography classes were productive.
No one **told** me Sharon's mother died last week.
Adam **told** us a pack of lies.

PAY ATTENTION!
READ CAREFULLY THE FOLLOWING SENTENCES IN THE PRESENT PERFECT SIMPLE.

She **hasn't told** me yet about her plans.
Bruna **has told** me the difference between the two methods.
Have you **told** your family about your dissatisfaction?
She **has** just **told** the same joke again!
Raymond **has told** me a surreal story about the origins of the village.

80. THINK THOUGHT THOUGHT

PAY ATTENTION!
READ CAREFULLY THE FOLLOWING SENTENCES IN THE PAST SIMPLE.

Deborah **thought** I was lying.
'It doesn't matter', he **thought** to himself.
Dora **thought** I had handled the situation in a sensible way.
I really **thought** the first answer was right.
We **thought** Clive would be waiting for us.

PAY ATTENTION!
READ CAREFULLY THE FOLLOWING SENTENCES IN THE PRESENT PERFECT SIMPLE.

Have you **thought** about it yet?
I **have thought** about the useful suggestions that you made.
She **has** always **thought** of herself as a confident person.
Pauline **has thought** about living in Denmark.
Austin **has thought** of becoming a vegetarian.

81. THROW THREW THROWN

> **PAY ATTENTION!**
> **READ CAREFULLY THE FOLLOWING SENTENCES IN THE PAST SIMPLE.**

Sylvia **threw** a snowball at me.
I **threw** my jacket on the chair.
She **threw** a lot of money on the desk.
Andrew **threw** two pillows to me.
He **threw** Clarice her towel.

> **PAY ATTENTION!**
> **READ CAREFULLY THE FOLLOWING SENTENCES IN THE PRESENT PERFECT SIMPLE.**

Someone **has thrown** a stone at the door.
Leonardo **has thrown** his clothes on the sofa.
I **have** just **thrown** away the old magazines.
Since his wife died, he **has thrown** himself into his work.
Have you ever **thrown** a surprise party ?

PRACTICE MAKES PERFECT

17.1 Complete the senteces with the past simple of the verbs in the box. Use each verb twice.

TEACH	TEAR	TELL	THINK	THROW

a) Gregory _____ me he was having a 40 minute walk every evening.

b) The strike _____ the transport system into chaos.

c) "He's very observant", I _____ to myself.

d) Selma _____ herself languages.

e) My youngest son _____ a hole in my raincoat.

f) My boss _____ me that I would be promoted.

g) Look at this! Your lovely pet _____ my rug!

h) Albert Einstein _____ physics in Switzerland and Germany.

i) Gordon _____ it necessary to see an eye specialist.

j) The singer _____ a CD to the fans in the rock concert.

IRREGULAR VERBS: THE ULTIMATE GUIDE

17.2 Turn the sentences into the interrogative form.

a) Mercedez taught Spanish at a public school.

_____?

b) The dog tore the shopping bag.

_____?

c) He told them about the terms and conditions of the contract.

_____?

d) Janine thought twice before making such an important decision.

_____?

e) Will threw away the chance to study at Stanford University.

_____?

17.3 Turn these sentences into the negative form.

a) My mother taught me to read when I was four.

   _____.

b) I tore a pile of leaflets.

   _____.

c) Stephen told me you got divorced.

   _____.

d) Judy thought her tight clothes were attractive.

   _____.

e) The boys threw the ball back and forth.

   _____.

Now check your answers by looking at the *Key to Exercises*.

17.4 Complete the sentences in the present perfect simple using the verbs in brackets.

a) Denzel (teach) _____ me the basics of computer programming.

b) Ruth (tear) _____ the photograph out of the album.

c) (tell) _____ Aline _____ the truth to the police?

d) James is greedy and (think) _____ big since he was a teenager.

e) No one realised they (throw) _____ the dice twice.

f) I (teach) _____ my children good citizens help to build a better society.

g) The candidates became nervous and (tear) _____ the application form.

h) (tell) _____ they _____ you exactly what's going on in the company?

i) He (think) _____ always _____ of himself as a talented painter.

j) I (throw) _____ up everything I had eaten.

k) David (teach/not) _____ Bruce any card tricks.

l) He (tear) _____ a muscle in his arm.

m) Douglas (tell) _____ me to make the most of my cooking skills.

n) Kile and I (think) _____ it possible to start a new life in South America.

o) Witney (throw) _____ the engagement ring back in my face.

Now check your asnwers by looking at the *Key to Exercises*.

UNIT 18
UNDERSTAND/WAKE/WEAR/WIN/WRITE

82. UNDERSTAND UNDERSTOOD UNDERSTOOD

> **PAY ATTENTION!**
> READ CAREFULLY THE FOLLOWING SENTENCES IN THE PAST SIMPLE.

I really **understood** your point of view about Donald Trump.

She was the only person who **understood** how I felt.

I'm sorry, but I **understood** you were not interested in sports.

Charlotte **understood** why I didn't donate money to the campaign.

It seems Stella **understood** the basic concepts of geometry.

> **PAY ATTENTION!**
> READ CAREFULLY THE FOLLOWING SENTENCES IN THE PRESENT PERFECT SIMPLE.

Alan **hasn't understood** the complex equation.

Rosalind **has understood** me perfectly well.

Have you u**nderstood** the bar graph?

Tim **hasn't understood** most of the statements.

You don't need to explain it again. I **have** already **understood** the main topic of the passage.

83. WAKE WOKE WOKEN

PAY ATTENTION!
READ CAREFULLY THE FOLLOWING SENTENCES IN THE PAST SIMPLE.

When she **woke** up, everyone was still asleep.
Penny **woke** me up as soon as breakfast was ready.
I **woke** up late yesterday morning.
Gabriel **woke** up when he heard a scream.
Monique slept peacefully and **woke** up feeling well.

PAY ATTENTION!
READ CAREFULLY THE FOLLOWING SENTENCES IN THE PRESENT PERFECT SIMPLE.

You **have** just **woken** up the baby!
Mick **has woken** to the sound of raindrops.
Andressa **hasn't woken** up yet.
Daniel and I **have woken** up early today.
Pat **has woken** up to the fact that he can overcome such obstacles.

84. WEAR WORE WORN

> **PAY ATTENTION!**
> READ CAREFULLY THE FOLLOWING SENTENCES IN THE PAST SIMPLE.

Brad **wore** a grey suit when I saw him two days ago.
I **wore** glasses when I was a child.
The queen **wore** a lilac hat during the religious ceremony.
Some applicants **wore** casual clothes for the interview.
He **wore** a green T-shirt and a cap.

> **PAY ATTENTION!**
> READ CAREFULLY THE FOLLOWING SENTENCES IN THE PRESENT PERFECT SIMPLE.

Have you **worn** your Italian shoes yet?
Ben **hasn't worn** the jacket I gave him.
Have you ever **worn** a work uniform?
The actress **has worn** a wig to play the leading role.
Mary and Marina **have worn** heavy make-up to look older.

85. WIN WON WON

PAY ATTENTION!
READ CAREFULLY THE FOLLOWING SENTENCES IN THE PAST SIMPLE.

The British cyclist Chris Froome **won** the Tour de France in 2017.
The measures **won** the approval of the board of directors.
Gisele **won** the talent show *Rising Star* in 2013.
The Celtics **won** the NBA title in 2009.
Mother Teresa **won** the Nobel Peace Prize in 1979.

PAY ATTENTION!
READ CAREFULLY THE FOLLOWING SENTENCES IN THE PRESENT PERFECT SIMPLE.

Our team **has** just **won** five matches in a row.
He **has won** an award for the protection of the environment.
Gill is so lucky! He **has** already **won** the lottery twice.
Finally Lucy **has won** the respect of her colleagues.
Have you ever **won** a large amount of money?

86. WRITE WROTE WRITTEN

> **PAY ATTENTION!**
> **READ CAREFULLY THE FOLLOWING SENTENCES IN THE PAST SIMPLE.**

Ernest Hemingway **wrote** many novels in the 1930s.

Richard **wrote** some e-mails this morning.

Leo Tolstoy **wrote** *Anna Karenina* in 1877.

Julie was in love and **wrote** love letters to her boyfriend every day.

The journalist Tom Wolf **wrote** collections of articles and essays.

> **PAY ATTENTION!**
> **READ CAREFULLY THE FOLLOWING SENTENCES IN THE PRESENT PERFECT SIMPLE.**

My sister **has written** a best-seller.

Jo **has written** the numbers on the board.

Gilbert **has written** a script for a TV programme.

They **have written** a weak concluding paragraph.

I **have** just **written** Carol a message telling her I would be late for dinner.

PRACTICE MAKES PERFECT

18.1 Complete the sentences with the past simple of the verbs below. Use each verb twice.

| UNDERSTAND | WAKE | WEAR | WIN | WRITE |

a) Warren _____ a long beard when I met him.

b) My family _____ my reaction.

c) British women _____ the right to vote in 1918.

d) Valerie _____ an expensive necklace when I met her.

e) Denzel _____ me up at 5 a.m.

f) Marlon _____ the situation completely.

g) Ricky Martin _____ the autobiography *Me* in 2010.

h) Chelsea Football Club _____ the Champions League in 2012.

i) At that time the Spanish chef _____ a cookbook.

j) The strange noise _____ everyone around 4 a.m.

18.2 Turn these sentences into the interrogative form.

a) Lesly understood all the rules of the game.

_____?

b) Fred woke up to the sound of a thunder.

_____?

c) Roberta wore a summer dress to the party.

_____?

d) England won the World Cup in 1966.

_____?

e) Lucy wrote about her experiences working as a volunteer.

_____?

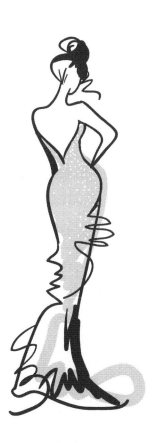

18.3 Turn these sentences into the negative form.

a) You understood what Claire intended to do.

_____.

b) She woke me up as soon as the home alarm system went off.

_____.

c) Shirley wore a blue dress to the cocktail.

_____.

d) The Italian actress won the Oscar in 1964.

_____.

e) Corina wrote down the winner's name.

_____.

Now check your answers by looking at the *Key to Exercises*.

18.4 Complete the sentences in the present perfect simple using the verbs in brackets.

a) He has a very strong accent, but I (understand) _____ each word he said.

b) The ambulance siren (wake) _____ all of them.

c) I (wear) _____ never _____ glasses for reading.

d) How many times (win) _____ Meryl Streep _____ the Oscar?

e) I know the girl who (write) _____ the lyrics of such a wonderful song!

f) I (understand/not) _____ that quote by Carl Yung.

g) The baby (wake) _____ many times during the night.

h) I (wear/not) _____ my new watch yet.

i) Vanessa (win) _____ a reputation for being radical.

j) Professor Mendel (write) _____ a biography of Winston Churchill.

k) (understand) _____ Ursula _____ your attitude?

l) It's time to leave, but Larissa (wake/not) _____ yet.

m) She (wear) _____ never _____ a piece of jewellery.

n) Martin wasn't fit and (win/not) _____ the race.

o) The students (write) _____ an essay about the philosopher Bertrand Russel.

Now check your answers by looking at the *Key to Exercises*.

ADDITIONAL EXERCISES

1.1 Complete the sentences with the verb <u>To Be</u> in the past simple.

a) William Faulkner _____ a great American writer.

b) Conrad and I _____ busy when Berta phoned us.

c) Jodie _____ the best student in her class last term.

d) This time last month Hugo and Gael _____ in Chile.

e) The food _____ good, but I didn't eat a lot.

f) Ervin and Elle _____ kind to us.

g) The accident _____ next to my house.

h) Edmund and Elise _____ the happiest couple I met in Ireland.

i) It _____ a lovely weekend.

j) I _____ on time for the appointment.

1.2 Turn these sentences into the interrogative form.

a) Miriam was in Rome last month.
_____?

b) Fernando and Frida were overjoyed at the news.
_____?

c) The weather was fine that morning.
_____?

d) Your children were at school at 5.30 p.m.
_____?

e) It was a new challenge for all of them.
_____?

1.3 Turn these sentences into the negative form.

a) The guests were at ease.
_____.

b) The sky was cloudy.
_____.

c) Ivonne was a short fat woman.
_____.

d) Joanna was ill two weeks ago.
_____.

e) Grace was in Monaco last month.
_____.

1.4 Fill in the blanks with the present perfect simple of the verb To Be.

a) We _____ twice to Sharon's house during this week.

b) The stores _____ packed because of the sales.

c) The exams (not) _____ easy, but our grades are better than ever!

d) Joshua _____ sick in the past week.

e) I _____ never _____ to Chicago.

f) _____ you ever _____ to Saudi Arabia?

g) Dimitri _____ away in the last three weeks.

h) Annette _____ lonely since her husband died.

i) Nathan _____ worried about his future.

j) I (not) _____ to the beauty shop today.

1.5 Put the verbs in brackets into the past simple.

a) Italy (beat) _____ Portugal in the cup final.

b) Such plants (become) _____ the focus of research.

c) They (break) _____ the news to Ted.

d) The housewife (buy) _____ two packages of rice.

e) The lion (catch) _____ its prey.

f) I (choose) _____ to stay away from heavy foods.

g) Stan (come) _____ straight from the bus station.

h) Juliane (do) _____ an amazing job!

i) Magali (drive) _____ all the way from Boston to New York.

j) The ladies (drink) _____ a lot of sparkling wine.

k) We (eat) _____ tiramisu for dessert.

l) The fabric (feel) _____ soft.

m) I (find) _____ Alan great company!

n) Joffrey (get) _____ frustrated when he checked the final score.

o) Warren (give) _____ the impression he had a crush on you!

p) Abel (have) _____ red hair and brown eyes.

q) We (keep) _____ telling ourselves everything was going well.

r) When I was 17, I (know) _____ nothing about life.

s) Groven (lose) _____ his wife a long time ago.

t) They (make) _____ their own clothes.

u) I (meet) _____ them when I went around the block.

v) I'm sure they (read) _____ the whole chapter.

w) She (say) _____ touching words that made us cry.

x) Ariel (see) _____ the side effects of the medicine.

y) Muriel (speak) _____ English with a slight French accent.

z) I (think) _____ the same thing you did!

aa) Avril (understand) _____ the agreement when she read it for the second time.

ab) Hector (wake) _____ up this morning with a terrible hangover.

ac) Michael Phelps (win) _____ eight gold medals at 2008 Beijing Games..

ad) We (write) _____ love letters to each other very often.

1.6 Turn these sentences into the interrogative form.

a) She began to make progress in her studies.

_____?

b) They lent him a lot of money.

_____?

c) The hat fell in the mud.
_____?

d) Leo flew to Seoul to attend a conference.
_____?

e) He forgot to take out the trash.
_____?

f) She forgave Antoine for walking out on her.
_____?

g) She heard Olive play the flute.
_____?

h) Benjamin left the motorway at Junction 12.
_____?

i) The study built a picture of the present situation.
_____?

j) Percy meant to irritate us.
_____?

1.7 Turn these sentences into the negative form.

a) Fleas bit our cats.
_____.

b) The experts brought the issue to light.
_____.

c) The sliding door stood open.
_____.

d) She cut her foot on a piece of glass.
   _____.

e) He drew a sketch of his flat.
   _____.

f) She fought to keep the family together.
   _____.

g) Malcom put the message across clearly.
   _____.

h) I shook the sand out of my slippers.
   _____.

i) The bell rang at the end of each lesson.
   _____.

j) We rode a bus back to Geneva that night.
   _____.

1.8 Complete the sentences in the present perfect simple using the verbs in brackets.

a) Lee took the texbook collections and (blow) _____ the dust off them.

b) The hotel suite (cost) _____ the earth!

c) We (hang) _____ up the Saint Patrick ornaments.

d) She (have) _____ headaches over the past weeks.

e) Edgar (hide) _____ the bottle of gim behind the jar.

f) The hammer (hit) _____ the ground hard.

g) The yen and the euro (hold) _____ steady lately.

h) He tripped and (hurt) _____ his ankle.

i) Charlize (go) _____ skydiving on her 90th birthday!

j) The city (grow) _____ in size over the years.

k) Bernard (let/not) _____ the opportunity pass him by.

l) Such matter (lie) _____ at the centre of the conflict.

m) Nigel (light) _____ the pipe.

n) I (pay) _____ them in pounds.

o) The rebels (rise) _____ up against such a political system.

p) The murderer (run) _____ away from the scene of the crime.

q) The users (send) _____ the feedback on our services.

r) Finally I (sell) _____ him my shares.

s) They (set/not) _____ the boxes on the floor.

t) She (show) _____ off her diploma in business management.

u) I turned the lights off and (shut) _____ the blinds.

v) Esther (sleep) _____ with the lights on.

w) She (stand/not) _____ back to let me in.

x) Ivory Coast (strike) _____ first with a goal in the second minute.

y) An innovative idea (take) _____ shape in my mind.

z) He (teach) _____ that we always need one another.

aa) I (tell) _____ them not to touch my clothes.

ab) The parliament (throw) _____ out the bill.

ac) Such cartoon characters (win) _____ the hearts and minds of an entire generation.

ad) The British author Ken Follet (write) _____ many novels over the years.

KEY TO EXERCISES

UNIT 1

1.1
a) was
b) was
c) were
d) was
e) were
f) was
g) was
h) were
i) were
j) was

1.2
a) Were Susan and Ashley close friends?
b) Were the packages heavy?
c) Was Carol very interested in politics?
d) Were the shops closed at lunchtime?
e) Were Jim and Morgan excellent golf players?

1.3
a) Your lipstick wasn't in your bag.
b) Nina and Naomi weren't well-dressed.
c) It wasn't a magic day for all of them.
d) Michael and Kate weren't together celebrating the New Year.
e) Nadia wasn't a very rational person.

1.4
a) have you been
b) has been
c) hasn't been
d) has Ronald been
e) haven't been
f) has been
g) have never been
h) have been
i) Has Clarice ever been
j) hasn't been
k) haven't been
l) has been
m) has been
n) have been
o) has been

UNIT 2

2.1
a) became
b) bit
c) beat
d) blew
e) began
f) blew
g) became
h) began
i) bit
j) beat

2.2
a) Did he beat Andrew in the last swimming race?
b) Did Alice become curious about astrology?
c) Did the meeting begin on time?
d) Did the dog bite Sylvia on the arm?
e) Did Arnold blow out the candles?

2.3
a) They didn't beat us in the final round of the world championship.

b) Sandra didn't become a top model in 2015.
c) The interview didn't begin at 9 a.m.
d) Margaux didn't bite the doughnut slowly.
e) Dorothy didn't blow up the yellow balloons.

2.4
a) have beaten
b) has become
c) has begun
d) has bitten
e) has blown
f) haven't beaten
g) have just become
h) have begun
i) hasn't bitten
j) have blown
k) Has Russia beaten
l) have become
m) Has the lecture begun
n) have bitten
o) has blown

UNIT 3

3.1
a) brought
b) bought
c) broke
d) brought
e) built
f) caught
g) broke
h) caught
i) bought
j) built

3.2
a) Did the printer break down again?
b) Did the research bring a fresh look to the topic?
c) Did they build the cathedral in the 18th century?
d) Did Josh buy a gold bracelet?
e) Did the FBI agents catch the terrorists?

3.3
a) Will didn't break his middle finger.
b) Pablo didn't bring home his Portuguese workmates.
c) They didn't build a luxury hotel near the sports centre.
d) Sophia didn't buy Karen a nighdress.
e) Claudia and Britney didn't catch a movie the other day.

3.4
a) has broken
b) have brought
c) hasn't built
d) have bought
e) has caught
f) has broken
g) have brought
h) has built
i) has bought
j) has caught
k) has broken
l) have you brought
m) has built
n) haven't bought
o) has the cat caught

UNIT 4

4.1
a) cut
b) chose
c) did
d) came
e) cost
f) did
g) cut
h) chose
i) came
j) cost

4.2
a) Did they choose to live in a quiet neighbourhood?
b) Did the circus come to town last spring?
c) Did the Easter egg cost ten pounds?
d) Did Beatrice cut herself chopping carrots?
e) Did the doctors do everything possible to save Gail?

4.3
a) I didn't choose a lively wallpaper for the living room.
b) Debra didn't come by our shop.
c) My dental treatment didn't cost me $3,000.
d) Ellon didn't cut precisely along the dotted lines.
e) Fred didn't do the washing slowly.

4.4
a) haven't chosen
b) has finally come
c) have cost
d) has cut
e) has done
f) has chosen
g) has never come
h) has cost
i) has cut
j) has Margareth done...?
k) has chosen
l) has come
m) have cost
n) has cut
o) has done

UNIT 5

5.1
a) drove
b) drew
c) drank
d) ate
e) fell
f) drank
g) drew
h) ate
i) fell
j) drove

5.2
a) Did Erika draw tropical birds?
b) Did Ron and Fred drink a bottle of white wine?
c) Did they drive back to Cardiff?
d) Did Joy and Raymond eat out yesterday evening?
e) Did Mick fall on the pavement?

5.3
a) Alison didn't draw wild animals.
b) Sean didn't drink three cups of coffee this morning.
c) Wayne didn't drive Claire to the airport.
d) They didn't eat a tasty fruit salad after having lunch.
e) Temperatures didn't fall below zero in the second week of December.

5.4
a) has drawn
b) has never drunk
c) has driven
d) have eaten
e) have fallen
f) have drawn
g) has drunk
h) have driven
i) has eaten
j) hasn't fallen
k) have you ever drawn
l) have you drunk
m) has driven
n) have never eaten
o) has fallen

UNIT 6

6.1
a) felt
b) forgot
c) fought
d) flew
e) flew
f) felt
g) forgot
h) fought
i) found
j) found

6.2
a) Did he feel great after the trip?
b) Did Arnold fight in Vietnam in 1971?
c) Did she find an experienced employee to replace Stan?
d) Did they fly Lufthansa?
e) Did Mel forget to pay the phone bill?

6.3
a) I didn't feel relaxed after having a walk.
b) Gabriel didn't fight with his neighbour.
c) I didn't find that soap opera confusing.
d) The doves didn't fly to the north at sunrise.
e) Carol and I didn't forget to invite Emily to the barbecue.

6.4
a) has felt
b) have fought
c) have found
d) have they flown
e) have you forgotten
f) has never felt
g) have fought
h) has found
i) have you ever flown
j) has never forgotten
k) have felt
l) has fought
m) have found
n) haven't flown
o) has forgotten

UNIT 7

7.1
a) grew
b) went
c) got
d) forgave
e) gave
f) grew
g) went
h) got
i) gave
j) forgave

7.2
a) Did Chris forgive his brother for such a bad behaviour?
b) Did Ed get a post as a marketing director?
c) Did the nurse give him an injection?
d) Did Ryan go to a pizzeria?
e) Did Enrico grow up playing different sports?

7.3
a) Nicky didn't forgive his girlfriend for being unfaithful to him.
b) I didn't get on the train at Bristol station.
c) George didn't give the supervisor a creative solution to the problem.
d) Rachel didn't go to the Louvre Museum twice last month.
e) The Mexican economy didn't grow 2% in 2017.

7.4
a) has forgiven
b) has got
c) has given
d) have gone
e) haven't grown
f) hasn't forgiven
g) have they got
h) has given
i) have just gone
j) has grown
k) hasn't forgiven
l) have got
m) has given
n) have you gone
o) has grown

UNIT 8

8.1
a) had
b) hid
c) hit
d) hung
e) heard
f) hung
g) hit
h) had
i) hit
j) heard

8.2
a) Did they hang out last Saturday night?
b) Did Hilton have a Lamborghini many years ago?
c) Did Michelle hear them go out?

IRREGULAR VERBS: THE ULTIMATE GUIDE

d) Did Martin hide evidence from the jury?
e) Did he hit the ball as hard as he could?

8.3
a) Catherine didn't hang the overcoat on the hook.
b) The couple didn't have three children.
c) We didn't hear Meg's voice.
d) Stephania didn't hide the coupons underneath the pillow.
e) Prices didn't hit rock bottom.

8.4
a) have hung
b) hasn't had
c) hasn't heard
d) have the criminals hidden
e) have never hit
f) has hung
g) hasn't had
h) has heard
i) has Vladimir hidden
j) has hit
k) has hung
l) have had
m) have heard
n) has hidden
o) has hit

UNIT 9

9.1
a) held
b) knew
c) hurt
d) left
e) kept
f) held
g) hurt
h) kept
i) knew
j) left

9.2
a) Did they hold a reception to welcome the British ambassador?
b) Did Keanu hurt his arm playing handball?
c) Did Francine keep up with her studies?
d) Did Sonia know the risks of the surgery?
e) Did the bus leave the station fifteen minutes late?

9.3
a) The National Museum didn't hold an exhibition of Salvador Dali's work in January.
b) It didn't hurt me to hear that Liz was insensitive about the matter.
c) Louise didn't keep herself out of trouble.
d) Joseph didn't know Peter was a talented architect.
e) Martin didn't leave work at 6.15 p.m.

9.4
a) has held
b) have hurt
c) has kept
d) have you known
e) has left
f) have held

g) has hurt
h) have the artists kept...?
i) have known
j) has left
k) have held
l) has Tim hurt
m) have kept
n) have known
o) has left

UNIT 10

10.1
a) let
b) lit
c) lent
d) lost
e) lay
f) let
g) lost
h) lent
i) lay
j) lit

10.2
a) Did the bank lend the company a great deal of money?
b) Did they let Gregory decide what to do?
c) Did Liz lie down for a while on the sofa?
d) Did Ivan light the campfire?
e) Did Boris lose the sight in one eye?

10.3
a) Nick didn't lend Paul a notepad.
b) I didn't let them eat fatty food.
c) Deryl didn't lie back in the chair.
d) They didn't light up the statue.
e) The clerk didn't lose his temper with the stubborn customer.

10.4
a) has lent
b) has let
c) have lain
d) hasn't lit
e) has she lost
f) has lent
g) have you let
h) has just lain
i) has lit
j) have you lost
k) has lost
l) has let
m) has lain
n) have lit
o) has lent

UNIT 11

11.1
a) met
b) made
c) made
d) paid
e) put
f) meant
g) paid
h) meant
i) met
j) put

11.2
a) Did Ryan make the most of the weekend at the campsite?
b) Did your commitment mean better days for all of them?
c) Did they meet tourists from all over the world last summer?
d) Did Walt pay the tablet by credit card?
e) Did Raissa put the kids to bed around eleven o'clock?

11.3
a) Glenda didn't make a fuss about the parking fine.
b) Melania didn't mean to cheat you.
c) Susan and Sidney didn't meet at college.
d) They didn't pay a visit to the medieval cathedral.
e) Emily didn't put herself in an embarassing situation.

11.4
a) has meant
b) hasn't meant
c) have met
d) has she paid
e) have put
f) has made
g) has meant
h) have already met
i) have paid
j) has put
k) has made
l) have made
m) has the German prime minister met
n) haven't paid
o) have you put

UNIT 12

12.1
a) rode
b) rose
c) read
d) ran
e) rang
f) read
g) rode
h) rose
i) ran
j) rang

12.2
a) Did Joyce read a report about climate change?
b) Did Carry ride the subway every day last week?
c) Did Ronda ring back as soon as she found the voucher?
d) Did the unemployment rate rise in many European countries at that time?
e) Did they run out of gas?

12.3
a) Cindy didn't read a short story by Jack London.
b) The kids didn't ride the merry-go-round.

c) Spencer didn't ring the company to get more information about the job.
d) The birth rate didn't rise last year.
e) Naomi didn't run towards the gate.

12.4
a) has read
b) hasn't ridden
c) have rung
d) has risen
e) has run
f) have you read
g) has never ridden
h) has rung
i) have the sales risen...
j) has run
k) has read
l) have ridden
m) have you rung
n) have risen
o) has run

UNIT 13

13.1
a) sold
b) saw
c) said
d) set
e) sent
f) set
g) said
h) saw
i) sold
j) sent

13.2
a) Did she say a prayer for the missing miners?
b) Did Yan see Shirley walking around the square?
c) Did Eike sell his private jet?
d) Did they send Scott a computer file?
e) Did Maryah set a trap to catch the coyote?

13.3
a) She didn't say Keith would come back.
b) Annabel didn't see the task as a challenge.
c) John didn't sell his cottage in 2015.
d) I didn't send Ruy a thank-you letter.
e) Carlo didn't set to work to fix the computers.

13.4
a) has said
b) have seen
c) has sold
d) hasn't sent
e) has never set
f) has said
g) have seen
h) has sold
i) have you sent
j) has set
k) has said
l) has seen
m) have sold
n) have you sent
o) has set

UNIT 14

14.1

a) shut
b) showed
c) shut
d) shook
e) shot
f) showed
g) shot
h) shook
i) shone
j) shone

14.2

a) Did the senator and the mayor shake hands?
b) Did the stars shine brightly last night?
c) Did they shoot the movie in Greece?
d) Did Hilton show them how to use the database software?
e) Did Andrew shut the back door?

14.3

a) The ground didn't shake violently.
b) The street lights didn't shine along the avenue.
c) He didn't shoot me an angry look.
d) Christian didn't show talent for writing fiction.
e) They didn't shut the door behind them.

14.4

a) has shaken
b) has shone
c) have shot
d) has shown
e) have shut
f) has shaken
g) has shone
h) have shot
i) has shown
j) has the director shot
k) has shaken
l) have shone
m) has just shut
n) has shown
o) has shut

UNIT 15

15.1

a) slept
b) spoke
c) sang
d) spent
e) sat
f) spent
g) sang
h) slept
i) sat
j) spoke

15.2

a) Did dad sing a song by 'The Beatles'?
b) Did the little girl sit down to watch cartoons?
c) Did Christine sleep on the sofa?
d) Did they speak about their professions?
e) Did Wanderson spend a lot of money on himself?

15.3
a) Thomas didn't sing all night long.
b) They didn't sit down to discuss the new policy.
c) I didn't sleep late last Sunday.
d) Serena didn't speak clearly and slowly.
e) The previous administration didn't spend billions of dollars on health care services.

15.4
a) has sung
b) has never slept
c) has sat
d) have you spoken
e) has spent
f) has sung
g) has sat
h) hasn't slept
i) hasn't spoken
j) have spent
k) have sung
l) have sat
m) has just slept
n) have spoken
o) has spent

UNIT 16

16.1
a) stood
b) stole
c) swam
d) took
e) struck
f) struck
g) swam
h) stood
i) took
j) stole

16.2
a) Did Frank stand out in the job market?
b) Did Rick steal the scene again?
c) Did the SUV strike a lorry?
d) Did she swim in the Pacific Ocean?
e) Did they take your experience into account?

16.3
a) Marcia didn't stand close to the huge tree.
b) The robbers didn't steal computers and TV sets.
c) The boat didn't strike a large rock.
d) Sonia didn't swim every single day when she lived by the sea.
e) Gordon didn't take care of the children when his wife was away.

16.4
a) have stood
b) has stolen
c) have struck
d) have you ever swum
e) haven't taken
f) has stood
g) has stolen
h) has struck
i) have swum
j) has took
k) has stood
l) have they stolen
m) has struck

n) has swum
o) have taken

UNIT 17

17.1
a) told
b) threw
c) thought
d) taught
e) tore
f) told
g) tore
h) taught
i) thought
j) threw

17.2
a) Did Mercedez teach Spanish at a public school?
b) Did the dog tear the shopping bag?
c) Did he tell them about the terms and conditions of the contract?
d) Did Janine think twice before making such an important decision?
e) Did Will throw away the chance to study at Stanford University?

17.3
a) My mother didn't teach me to read when I was four.
b) I didn't tear a pile of leaflets.
c) Stephen didn't tell me you got divorced.
d) Judy didn't think her tight clothes were attractive.
e) The boys didn't throw the ball back and forth.

17.4
a) has taught
b) has torn
c) has Aline told
d) has thought
e) have thrown
f) have taught
g) have torn
h) have they told
i) has always thought
j) have thrown
k) hasn't taught
l) has torn
m) has told
n) have thought
o) has thrown

UNIT 18

18.1
a) wore
b) understood
c) won
d) wore
e) woke
f) understood
g) wrote
h) won
i) wrote
j) woke

18.2
a) Did Leslie understand all the rules of the game?

b) Did Fred wake up to the sound of a thunder?
c) Did Roberta wear a summer dress to the party?
d) Did England win the World Cup in 1966?
e) Did Mel write about her experiences working as a volunteer?

18.3
a) You didn't understand what Claire intended to do.
b) She didn't wake me up as soon as the home alarm system went off.
c) Shirley didn't wear a blue dress to the cocktail.
d) The Italian actress didn't win the Oscar in 1964.
e) Corina didn't write down the winner's name.

18.4
a) have understood
b) has woken
c) have never worn
d) has Meryl Streep won
e) has written
f) haven't understood
g) has woken
h) haven't worn
i) has won
j) has written
k) has Ursula understood
l) hasn't woken
m) has never worn
n) hasn't won
o) have written

ADDITIONAL EXERCISES

1.1
a) was
b) were
c) was
d) were
e) was
f) were
g) was
h) were
i) was
j) was

1.2
a) Was Miriam in Rome last month?
b) Were Fernando and Frida overjoyed at the news?
c) Was the weather fine that morning?
d) Were your children at school at 5.30 p.m.?
e) Was it a new challenge for all of them?

1.3
a) The guests weren't at ease.
b) The sky wasn't cloudy.
c) Ivonne wasn't a short fat woman.
d) Joanna wasn't ill two weeks ago.
e) Grace wasn't in Monaco last month.

1.4
a) have been
b) have been
c) haven't been
d) has been
e) have never been
f) have you ever been
g) has been
h) has been
i) has been
j) haven't been

1.5
a) beat
b) became
c) broke
d) bought
e) caught
f) chose
g) came
h) did
i) drove
j) drank
k) ate
l) felt
m) found
n) got
o) gave
p) had
q) kept
r) knew
s) lost
t) made
u) met
v) read
w) said
x) saw
y) spoke
z) thought
aa) understood
ab) woke
ac) won
ad) wrote

1.6

a) Did she begin to make progress in her studies?
b) Did they lend him a lot of money?
c) Did the hat fall in the mud?
d) Did Leo fly to Seoul to attend a conference?
e) Did he forget to take out the trash?
f) Did she forgive Antoine for walking out on her?
g) Did she hear Olive to play the flute?
h) Did Benjamin leave the motorway at Junction 12?
i) Did the study build a picture of the present situation?
j) Did Percy mean to irritate us?

1.7

a) Fleas didn't bite our cats.
b) The experts didn't bring the issue to light.
c) The sliding door didn't stand open.
d) She didn't cut her foot on a piece of glass.
e) He didn't draw the sketch of his flat.
f) She didn't fight to keep the family together.
g) Malcom didn't put the message across clearly.
h) I didn't shake the sand out of my slippers.
i) The bell didn't ring at the end of each lesson.
j) We didn't ride a bus back to Geneva that night.

1.8.

a) has blown
b) has cost
c) have hung
d) has had
e) has hidden
f) has hit
g) have held
h) has hurt
i) has gone
j) has grown
k) hasn't let
l) has lain
m) has lit
n) have paid
o) have risen
p) has run
q) have sent
r) have sold
s) haven't set
t) has shown
u) have shut
v) has slept
w) hasn't stood
x) has struck
y) has taken
z) has taught
aa) have told
ab) has thrown
ac) have won
ad) have written

BE WAS/WERE BEEN	FALL FELL FALLEN
BEAT BEAT BEATEN	FEEL FELT FELT
BECOME BECAME BECOME	FIGHT FOUGHT FOUGHT
BEGIN BEGAN BEGUN	FIND FOUND FOUND
BITE BIT BITTEN	FLY FLEW FLOWN
BLOW BLEW BLOWN	FORGET FORGOT FORGOTTEN
BREAK BROKE BROKEN	FORGIVE FORGAVE FORGIVEN
BRING BROUGHT BROUGHT	GET GOT GOT
BUILD BUILT BUILT	GIVE GAVE GIVEN
BUY BOUGHT BOUGHT	GO WENT GONE
CATCH CAUGHT CAUGHT	GROW GREW GROWN
CHOOSE CHOSE CHOSEN	HANG HUNG HUNG
COME CAME COME	HAVE HAD HAD
COST COST COST	HEAR HEARD HEARD
CUT CUT CUT	HIDE HID HIDDEN
DO DID DONE	HIT HIT HIT
DRAW DREW DRAWN	HOLD HELD HELD
DRINK DRANK DRUNK	HURT HURT HURT
DRIVE DROVE DRIVEN	KEEP KEPT KEPT
EAT ATE EATEN	KNOW KNEW KNOWN

LEAVE LEFT LEFT
LEND LENT LENT
LET LET LET
LIE LAY LAIN
LIGHT LIT LIT
LOSE LOST LOST
MAKE MADE MADE
MEAN MEANT MEANT
MEET MET MET
PAY PAID PAID
PUT PUT PUT
READ READ READ
RIDE RODE RIDDEN
RING RANG RUNG
RISE ROSE RISEN
RUN RAN RUN
SAY SAID SAID
SEE SAW SEEN
SELL SOLD SOLD
SEND SENT SENT
SET SET SET
SHAKE SHOOK SHAKEN
SHINE SHONE SHONE
SHOOT SHOT SHOT

SHOW SHOWED SHOWN
SHUT SHUT SHUT
SING SANG SUNG
SIT SAT SAT
SLEEP SLEPT SLEPT
SPEAK SPOKE SPOKEN
SPEND SPENT SPENT
STAND STOOD STOOD
STEAL STOLE STOLEN
STRIKE STRUCK STRUCK
SWIM SWAM SWUM
TAKE TOOK TAKEN
TEACH TAUGHT TAUGHT
TEAR TORE TORN
TELL TOLD TOLD
THINK THOUGHT THOUGHT
THROW THREW THROWN
UNDERSTAND UNDERSTOOD UNDERSTOOD
WAKE WOKE WOKEN
WEAR WORE WORN
WIN WON WON
WRITE WROTE WRITTEN